Th⋮

BYRD TO BRITTEN

HENRY PURCELL, 1659–1695
by John Closterman

Sydney Northcote

Byrd to Britten

A Survey of English Song

JOHN BAKER

5 ROYAL OPERA ARCADE,
PALL MALL, LONDON,
S.W.1.

© 1966
by Sydney Northcote.
First published 1966 by
John Baker Publishers Limited,
5 Royal Opera Arcade,
Pall Mall, London,
S.W.1.

Printed in Great Britain
by Unwin Brothers Limited
Woking and London

For Alec Redshaw, Esq.

Dear Alec,

  For a long time you have been urging me to write this book so it is right you should share some of the responsibility. I hope you will feel that our many discussions—I remember one on board ship during a storm in mid-Atlantic—have been justified. I know it could have been considerably extended but it would have been very difficult to have made it exhaustive. But if it is provocative enough to restore some faith, which you and I share, in the repute of English song, the labour will not have been in vain.

Croydon, 1966.   S.N.

Preface

IN attempting this survey of a given period of English song it must be admitted I am satisfying an ambition I have long cherished. As a one-time singer and teacher myself I always believed in the highest qualities of our native song despite the discouragement, and, indeed, disparagement of some colleagues and friends. This book, then, is not so much an academic essay as a declaration of faith, though not born of patriotism alone.

The choice of a suitable period for study was not difficult to decide and the alliterative title is not merely fanciful. After all, the glory of the German Lied might be contained within a similar sort of title—From Mozart to Marx—a shorter period which depended on a rare assemblage of poets and composers as well as the encouragement of what Arthur Jacobs has described as 'a public susceptible to the subtle matching of verse and music as the representation of an individual emotion'. It would be strange indeed if the consistent excellence of English lyric poetry, with a longer history than most poetry, did not, at some points, find composers to match it, even if, in the changing fabric of our social and cultural habits, it was not always easy to find the third requirement, an understanding and appreciative audience. And, of course, we must remember that not all the greatest songs are settings of the greatest poetry.

From another point of view, the alliterative title may be more fortuitous than it seems. William Byrd, so often and rather variously described as the 'father of our musicke', was one of the greatest musical figures in the first Elizabethan era. Not only did he leave more examples for voice and string accompaniment than his contemporaries but he was interested in the more prominent poets of his day and was not averse from odd and peculiar texts. Benjamin Britten, a distinguished composer of the second Elizabethan age, shares some of these characteristics with his predecessor; and he is certainly at his best when setting words to music. During the four centuries (almost) which separate them it must be conceded that English song has had a chequered history, at times rising to the greatest heights but sometimes falling to the depths of banality. Even so, there are not wanting some threads of artistic continuity (e.g. the Shakespeare songs of successive ages offer interesting comparisons); and there are moments, too, when some shining examples are in danger of being lost in the mediocrity which may surround them.

In general matters of musical history the reader is referred to Ernest Walker's *History of Music in England* (Oxford) which in its current (third) edition has been so superbly edited and extended by Prof. Sir Jack Westrup. It is surely unnecessary and indeed invidious for me to tread any of the same ground here. On the point of any international comparison *A History of Song* edited by Denis Stevens (Hutchinson) is eminently worth consulting. In the more limited scope of the present survey I have been more concerned with the social changes and cultural circumstances, many peculiar to this country, which sometimes brought strange pressures and demands to our song writers. And singers, too, at varying stages, were bound to influence matters to a certain degree. Also, there is the uncomfortable fact that, in all ages, the English, with an aggravating modesty, are so often prone to regard their musicians as second rate.

Inevitably, in a book of this kind, there is always the danger of the text reading too much like an annotated catalogue. I have tried to avoid this as far as possible by making my selections indicative rather than exhaustive and concentrating mainly on items which are fairly easily accessible. But this is not without its difficulty because so many songs, even recent ones like those of Warlock and Moeran, have been allowed to go 'out of print' for various reasons, though mainly, one suspects, because of lack of public interest. Nowadays, the song recital even by a singing star, would attract only a small minority; and one devoted to English song would fare worse still. If this little book could stimulate only a faint improvement of interest in the art of song generally and English song particularly it will have served a useful purpose.

I would here like to acknowledge my deep gratitude to Mr Edward Miller for his invaluable help in the preparation of the earlier chapters; to Mr Alec Redshaw for his close attention to the later chapters; to Mrs June Leafe and my daughter Sylvia for preparing the typescript. Also to The National Portrait Gallery, the Syndics of the Fitzwilliam Museum, the Trustees of the British Museum, Messrs J. M. Dent and Sons, and Novello and Co. for permission to use illustrations, as well as to Messrs Stainer and Bell Ltd for permission to use the musical example on page 35 and to the Trustees of the British Museum for the music examples on pages 78–9.

Croydon, 1965.   S.N.

A*

Contents

List of Plates

I
Introduction

IN an age when the words 'Song' and 'Singing' have such wildly different connotations it may be as well to examine some of the artistic elements of each. The art of setting words to music is at once skilful and sensitive and the problem has exercised men's minds for centuries. Merbecke's adoption of a special notation to express the syllabic values and accents in English; some of Morley's statements in his *Plain and Easy Introduction to Music*; Dante's *De Vulgaris Eloquentia*; the close association of poets and musicians in the first Elizabethan era; the characteristic observations of Purcell and of Milton are only a few indications, taken at random from the earlier times, of the thought given to the artistic problem. Similar discussions have gone on ever since down to the present day, even after the celebrated but non-existent Poetic Supremacy Act of 1887, which was Colles's critical jibe about the methods of Hugo Wolf. Manifestly, the art of song is not the comparatively simple affair that so many assume it to be.

Perhaps if we get back a little nearer to the source we will find that poetry and music were sister arts which, as it were, grew up together, each exercising considerable influence on the other. There are those, like Percy Scholes, who see in song an art of compromise. Others would probably classify it, with opera, as a hybrid art. The truth is that, in its origins at least, song was an art in itself. We have but to reflect that primitive poetry was always sung. The terms poet and musician were then more or less synonymous. The actual progress from simple folk-song to 'songs written with conscious art' is not easily traceable (at least not briefly) and varies from country to country. Moreover the one did not end when the other began.

This partly if not wholly explains why the gap between what we may term, for want of better epithets, the 'popular' and 'serious' in song was not so abysmally wide in earlier days as it is today. It is evident, too, that by the time musicians and poets had parted company, so to speak, they had already exchanged some fundamental ideas as to form, structure, expression, rhythm and so on of positive importance to each. They had forged their technical tools in the same fire, the natural inflexion and intonation of their mother tongue. From this arise the intrinsic differences in the folk music of different countries. I am only too conscious that the argument has been rather over-simplified and that I have omitted some important cross-currents, notably that of dance, but some of these points will arise later. Here my main purpose has been to show that the art of song originated in an impulse that was common to both music and poetry. Thus we can speak of the poetry of music and the music of poetry with reasonable clarity of thought even if the exact definitions may vary.

The Renaissance has been defined 'as a period and process of transition, fusion, preparation and tentative endeavour'. Its influence on the art of song was felt earlier and more extensively in Europe (and in France particularly) than in England. The English monarchy, in Denis Steven's words, preferred 'to regard secular music—like wine—as a necessarily imported product', and English composers tended to set their songs to French and Italian texts, some of which gained a certain European currency, as, for example, Dunstable's *O rosa bella*. There were also a few songs by English composers like Morton, Frye and Bedingham, set to English texts, which likewise found their way abroad and Manfred Bukofzer has an interesting account of what he calls the first English *chanson* on the Continent—*Princhesse of Youth*.[1] But it was perhaps true that England took the influence of the Renaissance and the Reformation simultaneously. At all events, the success and development of the Elizabethan ayre quickly made up the leeway and it may be that Caccini's *Nuove Musiche* was not as new as it seemed,

---

[1] See *Music and Letters*, Vol. XIX.

having been anticipated by the French (e.g., le Roy's *Airs de Cour*, 1573) and by the Elizabethans, in the publication of Dowland's *First Book of Ayres* (1597). The subsequent impact of Opera, the origins of which are conveniently dated 1600, was more immediate and widespread on European song than it was on English. There may be some significance in the fact that the public concert as an institution, providing for the performance of instrumental and vocal music, was an earlier development in England than on the Continent, so that the art of song became something more than the matter of 'chamber-music' which it was by origin.

Obviously, as the respective arts of music and poetry pursued their independent developments the technique of song writing was bound to get more and more complex, until it reached a point such as to justify Westrup's dictum that 'the just marriage of words and music is a problem for which it would be difficult to find a universal solution'. Difficult, certainly, but not, one hopes, impossible; and it is probable that solutions will be native rather than universal, as is exemplified by the characteristic differences between English Song, German *Lied*, French *Melodie*, and so on. I believe that English composers have sometimes met the problem with conspicuous success and a degree of consistency. When they have failed, more often than not it is because they have tried to set their native words with 'a foreign accent' as, for example, when the Mendelssohnian cult of the nineteenth century robbed so many of our composers of any originality in their vocal melody. It is significant, too, that indifferent music set to a great poem only debases the poetry but, on the other hand, some of the great masterpieces in song have been associated with an inferior quality of poetry. The classic example often quoted is Brahms's *Die Mainacht*. Other examples could, of course, be cited from Schubert and Schumann. But if the art of song sometimes seems unpredictable it is surely indispensable. Song people will have, whether it be what they deserve or what is imposed upon them.

It might be appropriate at this point to take a further look at the concert-giving vogue which began with the Restoration. This has nothing to do with the tavern entertainments which were familiar enough in Elizabethan times; nor was it

associated with the pre-Restoration music clubs referred to by
Pepys and Anthony Wood because these were apparently
concerned only with amateur participants. The growth of the
public concert was essentially professional and, arising from the
'centralisation of social life in London which followed the
resumption of Court activities'[1] was mainly metropolitan.
Audiences, drawn from the 'quality' were plentiful enough
although their behaviour was, at times, rather boorish. The
music was cosmopolitan and there are a few instances where
curiously non-musical novelties were introduced to draw the
crowd, even including lotteries, a strange precursor of the
bingo craze of today. Programmes of instrumental and vocal
music were rather haphazardly arranged and some of the
concerts were often untidy and, sometimes, unseemly. But
there is no denying the great influence which they exerted on
the course of music generally in England. Tilmouth informs us
that 'at Banister's concerts [held in the Whitefriars Theatre in
1672] the performers were mercenary teachers, chiefly
foreigners, and indeed foreign musicians, for whom the King
had already shewn an open preference both in his chapel
music and in the band of violins [supplanting the viols], were
not slow to take advantage of the new opportunities offered by
the early development of concert-giving in this country'.[2]

The rise of an English school of singing was also to become an
important feature. If it was not so readily apparent in the
seventeenth century it was discernible enough, as in the songs
written by Purcell for Richard Leveridge, a bass singer who was
also a composer. In the words of Mollie Sands, 'throughout the
eighteenth century, all over Europe, Italian opera was the most
spectacular goal of vocal ambition. It was a vocal *lingua franca*,
so to speak. But side by side with it in each country was what
one might call a vernacular, which never died out and was
particularly healthy in England. . . . The English were as usual
averse from too much theory and mistrustful of the expert and
his technique; they put their faith in the natural, the forthright
and even the improvised.'[3]

[1] *Proc. Royal Mus. Ass.*, Vol. 84 1957/8, pp. 13 ff.
[2] *Ibid.*
[3] *Proc. of Royal Mus. Ass.*, 1943–44, p. 12.

The fears expressed by North and others that the growth of the professional concert would undermine amateur activities proved to be less serious than anticipated. The warm enthusiasm for amateur music-making was not abated. Indeed it was during this time that several musical institutions, some still existing, were founded; e.g. the Three Choirs Festival (1724), the Madrigal Society (c. 1740), the Royal Society of Musicians (1738), the Academy of Ancient Music (1710). So far as the vocal art was concerned this was important, for then, as now, vocal music depended at least as much on the amateur as on the professional for support. On the other hand, this new public challenge was met by the professionals with no little energy and enterprise; and the skills displayed by the travelling foreign musicians undoubtedly stimulated and improved native effort. There is another side to the argument of course; when the public become arbiters they can also be tyrants. Musicians began to think they were servants of a public which had to be pleased at all costs. So this was not so much the early loosening of the shackles of aristocratic patronage, which was to culminate in Beethoven's characteristic gesture, as it was the exchange of one master for another. The glamour of the 'star' performer began to exert its somewhat wayward influence. Public taste can be, and often is, capricious and wilful. It was destined to have its effect on English song for a considerable time.

But the gap between the frankly popular entertainment and the more serious pursuit of music was not then as great as it is today. Indeed it can be said with truth that musical entertainment in this, the twentieth century, reaches an abysmal low and is fast becoming 'a genre of music' that is 'in danger of ceasing to be music at all'. The reason for discussing it here is because, in many ways, it affects the vocal art more harmfully than it does any other facet of music. When one reflects that all this is now so widely and constantly disseminated by arrogant publicity and the powerful media of radio, records and television it is manifestly too significant to be ignored. At least let us cite some of the grosser vices which are bound to affect public taste to a dangerous degree. The current fashion of 'hotting-up' folk songs with rhythms which are unrecognisable is plain anarchy. All sensibility is lost in an uncontrolled stridency or buried in a leering sentimentality. Nor is there anything done to nurture the public interest in folk song by investing it with an exaggerated political bias and tonal crudity; particularly when this leads to a performing intensity accompanied by gestures, both facial and manual, which any actor would dismiss as utter 'ham'. And English is surely never improved with an American accent, real or pseudo. The music critic of *The Times* has rightly observed that 'since the decline of the music hall, England has taken her popular songs from the United States, either directly or by mimicry'.[1] And what respect or appreciation can the public feel for the subtle and sensitive technique of the song composer when they are so constantly regaled with lush singing underlaid with advertising slogans for soaps, sweets and cigarettes?

And what of the 'pop' singers, so called? Women, with a hoarse chest tone sing in a compass which is hardly feminine and with voices which are often strident and utterly unrefined. Men adopting what is a light baritone compass, are equally unyielding in tone quality and veer between a languid sentimentality and a vehement shouting. Neither sex seems capable of sustaining tone on a vowel sound—watch their mouths—and they appear to masticate their words between softened initial consonants and nasal final consonants which they reach far too soon in any case. Nor have they much sense of tonal projection; without the microphone many of them would be more or less inaudible. Many of them are incapable of expressing the trite sentiments of their words without meaningless gestures of hands and arms which are unnaturally strenuous. Their performance is the very antithesis of singing, the elements of which are founded on the progressive technique of centuries. In the days of the music hall, an entertainer like Harry Lauder, who could and did sing, was content to describe himself as a comedian. Why should these modern entertainers, even if their votive offerings from Mammon are so inordinately great, assume the title of singer, to which they are not entitled?

There is no denying that singing is able to serve as a useful and positive link between the light and serious in music,

[1] *The Times* (Music Critic) 27 December 1963.

especially in England which is essentially a singing nation,
drawing its strength from the influence of English words and
the long and splendid history of our Church music, despite one
or two stodgy periods. There is further evidence in the English
love of choral singing, an enthusiasm which has continued over
a very long period, reaching an almost unrivalled repute.
Moreover, song has always had the support of a vast army of
enthusiastic amateurs, even if the repertoire extends from the
highest achievements to items of lower artistic merit. At least
they have not degenerated to the more banal and barbaric
depths of some of the current vocal entertainment. And they do
honestly, though only partially, repel the invasion of the
drawing-room by radiogram and T.V. Prof. Westrup has
written eloquently of 'the influence that song has had on
English music. While in central Europe the popularity of the
Musikant has made instrumental music seem an obvious outlet,
in England the tradition of song has cast its spell on everything
we write. We glory in "The fine song for singing, the rare
song to hear!" This may have been at times a limitation, but it
has also proved a source of strength.'[1]

It is demonstrably true to say that the art of singing has often
been bedevilled by the claims of rival theories as well as by
some pseudo-science and a good deal of psychological jargon.
The saying that all one needs to know about singing can be
written on the back of a postcard is facetious; and the story of
the 'single page of exercises' which sufficed for Porpora to
teach the famous Caffarelli is probably apocryphal. The basic
principles of singing are not difficult to enumerate, whatever
methods are adopted to fulfil them. Obviously, the primary
essential is beauty of tone; 'for', as Hadow has said, 'in the first
place the function of music is to beautify and idealise'.[2] Allied
with this is the stern necessity for perfect intonation. It was Sir
Henry Wood who roundly declared that the chief requirement
of a singer was a 'good pair of ears'. Once having attained to
this tonal beauty the singer must then learn to sustain it, first
on a held-note evenly and also with controlled gradations of

[1] *The Character of England*, ed. Ernest Barker (Oxford 1950)
p. 407.
[2] *Collected Essays*, W. H. Hadow (Oxford), pp. 16–17.

tone. *Sostenuto* implies steadiness, a virtue often denied by an exaggerated *vibrato* which can so easily degenerate into an uncontrolled *tremolo*. Then there are two principles which were deemed 'twin pillars' by the old masters, *legato* and agility; in older terms, the pathetic and the florid, concerning which Mollie Sands has wisely remarked, 'the removal of one of them causes the structure [i.e., *bel canto*] to collapse'.[1] This rightly calls into question a certain current fashion, probably an exaggeration of the *baroque*, of singing *fioriture* with a thudding *staccato* incisiveness; about as logical as insisting that, for the sake of clarity, all passage-work in string music should be played with single bows. *Legato* may be principally a matter of vocal line and agility a question of a smooth suppleness, but both demand a subtle sense of rhythm. And as singers are mainly concerned with words, the purity and uniformity of vowel-sounds as well as the precision and clarity of consonants are matters of great concern. In this, perhaps, the 'resonator-scale' method of Dr W. A. Aiken and Sir Richard Paget is not without significance.

This is hardly the place to discuss the varied progress of the art of singing over the centuries and it may suffice to mention that the demands of composers at varying times have exercised a considerable influence; e.g. the operatic reforms of Gluck and Mozart halting some of the wilder excesses of *coloratura* or *canto figurato* and restoring something of the old *bel canto* style.[2] The great age of the *Lied* not only enhanced the prestige of German-speaking singers but also brought the challenge of a new intimacy and intellectual quality to singing. We shall find, too, that in the last half of the nineteenth century, English singers were less influenced by the intermittent operatic events of the times than they were by the more prevalent oratorio and concert-hall activities. As a result, the English style of singing is at its best in religious music and, on the evidence of the last sixty years or so, reveals a sympathetic aptitude for the more intimate kind of vocal music which is exemplified in solo song. There are those who feel that this renascence of song tended 'to

[1] *Groves Dictionary*, Vol. VII, p. 809.

[2] See the composite article on 'Singing', *Grove's Dictionary*, Vol. VII, p. 801 f.

exalt musical intelligence at the expense of more purely vocal qualities'.[1] This cannot be denied. We need to remind ourselves that interpretation alone, however convincing, is not real compensation for tonal or technical shortcomings. In any form of singing there is a minimum of technique below which no performance is really satisfactory. There is another danger which might be noted here. Our singers, both amateur and professional, are sometimes prone to attempt foreign languages before they have trained their vocal eloquence sufficiently in their mother tongue. Every language has its subtleties. Correct pronunciation is not enough, even if it is patterned on recorded performances of the particular item, because some of these may be good guides but not such good counsellors. Moreover, song is essentially a personal expression based on poetic understanding as well as musical appreciation.

The art of the song composer is not so easily summarised. Not only because it varies from age to age and from country to country, but also because it is, in many ways, a highly individual technique. To dismiss song as a slender form of music is not always defensible. Indeed, a good many composers who are eminently successful on the larger canvas of symphony and the like have been found to falter in their song writing. Elgar is perhaps an example, despite one or two successes. The technique is not merely a matter of reconciling the poetic syntax with the musical syntax; or of fusing rhythm and metre, stress and inflexion; nor yet the matter of a sensitive use of the vocal *tessitura*. Michael Tippett expresses something of the complexity of song writing when he says: 'As soon as we sing any poetry to a recognisable melody we have at that instant left the art of poetry for the art of music . . . we might even demonstrate by experiment the moment when chanted recitation of poetry hovers perhaps on the borderline between the two arts; the poetic listener still trying to appreciate the poetry, the musical listener already appreciating the chanting as music. Once the chanting has gone over into song, then our appreciation of the words virtually ceases.'[2] Tippett's prose, like his music, often

[1] Op. cit., p. 811.
[2] *A History of Song*, ed. Denis Stevens, p. 462.

seems more abstract than it is but these remarks of his carry the germ of an important idea.

This leads us to the elusive question of song forms. The *strophic*, in which the same melody serves for all the verses, is not as elementary as it may seem. Brahms used to say it was the most difficult. Perhaps it needs something of the uncanny genius of a Schubert. If we try to distinguish between the simple melodic type of song, the concentrated emotion of the lyrical mood, and the 'diffused force' of dramatic presentation, we are still confronted with a latitude of treatment which makes difficult any formal categorisation of the musical design. It has been said that because the hearer is guided by the sense of the words perhaps musical form seems of secondary importance. But only seems, because mere rhapsodising is hardly sufficient. Tovey's remarks on this question are interesting: 'It matters not whether the composer writes in self-sufficient musical form, or attends to the musical form without attending to the words, or attends to both and neither alternately; the moment words are heard or suspected, they inevitably become the key to the situation.'[1] Compare with Tippett's opinion quoted earlier. Not infrequently a song may seem to engender its own particular design which may reside in the vocal line, or in the accompaniment, or in both. For example, in *Dido's Lament* (Purcell), the accompaniment rests quite coherently on a ground bass while the vocal melody has its own independent design which is as perfectly balanced as it is superbly eloquent.

Tippett has said that 'response to situation is the primal gift of the song writer. Then comes the ability to destroy all the verbal music of the poetry and prose and to substitute the music of music.' This sounds more devastating than it is. There is an element of truth in it. But his suggestion that the response of the accompaniment to the poetic situation 'is at one or more remove'[2] is debatable. A song with orchestral accompaniment may have something of the lineaments of the operatic *scena*; but when the accompaniment is for strings or piano, song comes nearer to its natural function as chamber music. Undoubtedly

[1] *Essays in Musical Analysis* (Oxford), Vol. V.
[2] Op. cit., p. 466.

Schubert, Schumann and Brahms raised the art of song accompaniment to its highest achievements and later composers were ready enough to follow their example. English composers, too, from Parry and Stanford onwards, have not been found wanting in this particular skill and felicity.

Perhaps a brief digression may be allowed to glance at a reverse kind of song writing, when we find a poet like Thomas Moore adding new poetic texts to his native melodies with considerable success. A Welsh bard, Ceiriog, did much the same for his native folk song. And there is, of course, the lyric genius of Robert Burns in Scots songs. Indeed, there are some quite subtle examples of Burns's work in this direction as, for example, when he took a dance tune, a Strathspey, and after slowing down the tempo considerably was able to wed it with words which created a song of a very different nature in *Ca' the yowes*. On the other hand, the case of Darius Milhaud in setting the words of a trade catalogue to music is merely a bit of perverse frivolity; and not quite as good a joke as Robert Jones's madrigal (from his First Book) taking for a text publishers' tags used in printing a volume.

The future of English song will depend on composers, singers, teachers and public alike. Composers must beware of treating the voice only as a musical instrument. Song is a form of human eloquence and not merely an artistic abstraction. There are signs that the vocal recital is coming back to favour, but the public must be sure to go in order to listen to the songs and not just to hear a voice. And singers and teachers must show complete integrity for the composer's intentions and not indulge in improvised 'editing' just to get an isolated effect. Plunket Greene's epigram must not be forgotten: 'It is the composer who lives; the singer is one of the Ephemeridae.'[1]

[1] *Interpretation in Song*, H. Plunket Greene (Macmillan).

2

The First Elizabethan Age

NOT infrequently the tradition which is attributed to the first Elizabethan Age is that of a Merrie England, a bold, vigorous people united in utter loyalty to a spirited queen. In fact, a golden age when learning, literature and music flourished in abundance; when power and riches were accumulated by fearless adventurers as impudent as they were intrepid; when political ascendancy was won by an adroit and opportunist foreign policy. But this is little more than an enthusiastic gloss which omits so much that is important and ignores the many trials and tribulations of a most eventful reign. It is true that 'Elizabethan England, after two centuries powerful and wealthy, found time for the Renaissance'. Drama, cultivated by Udal, Sackville, Peel, Greene and Marlow culminated in the work of 'rare Ben Jonson' and, of course, the greatest genius of them all, William Shakespeare. There was, too, the poetry of Edmund Spenser, Philip Sidney, Gabriel Harvey and others; and in learning there was Roger Ascham's *Schoolmaster*, Hooker's *Of the Laws of Ecclesiastical Polity*, as well as Francis Bacon's *Advancement of Learning* and his *Novum Organum* as only some of the outstanding examples of the prevailing culture, to say nothing of the madrigalists and the lutenists. But we must remember, too, the religious and political conflicts of the times; and there is a significance in the passing of the Poor Law Act in 1601 which, with an amendment some sixty years later, continued in force until 1834.

Similarly, in considering the generic impulse behind Elizabethan music, and the *Ayre* particularly, we must be careful not to read too much into Chappell's remarks: 'Tinkers sang catches; milkmaids sang ballads; carters whistled; each trade, even the beggars, had their special songs.'[1] Then there is the other notion of the times that the 'compleat gentleman' must needs be able to sight-read and sustain his part in a madrigal. For all its hint of snobbishness it is probably true. But to infer from all these statements, as some have done, that madrigal singing was the normal pursuit of even a moderately large part of the populace is hardly tenable. Even the fact that a song like Dowland's *Now O now I needs must part* passed so soon into popular usage must not be taken out of context.[2] It does not imply any cross-fertilisation between the popular song and the aristocratic pursuits of the lutenists. Not even when we consider, for example, such things as the instrumental variations which Byrd wrote on *Sellenger's Round* and *The Carmen's Whistle*. It must not be forgotten that despite the up-growth of the grammar schools the majority of the people were illiterate. Of the many popular songs of the period we have fairly accurate information because of the references made to them by Shakespeare and other Elizabethan dramatists.

By contrast with the music, Elizabethan drama undoubtedly received its essential impetus from the populace. When the Earl of Leicester's servants erected the first public theatre in Shoreditch it set the stage for the most remarkable period of English drama. As Green has said: 'It was the people itself that created its Stage. The theatre, indeed, was commonly only the courtyard of an inn, or a mere booth . . . at a country fair; the bulk of the audience sat beneath the open sky in the "pit" or yard, a few covered seats in the galleries which ran round it formed the boxes of the wealthier spectators, while patrons and nobles found seats upon the actual boards.' He continues: 'Rude as the theatre might be, all the world was there. The stage was crowded with nobles and courtiers. Apprentices and citizens thronged the benches in the yard below. . . . No stage was ever so human, no poetic life so intense. Wild, reckless, defiant of all past tradition, of all conventional laws, the

[1] Chappell's *Old English Popular Music*.

[2] Whether Dowland adopted a known *Galliard* or his song became the popular *Frog Galliard* is not quite clear; but it does not invalidate my argument.

English dramatists owned no teacher, no source of poetic inspiration, but the People itself.'[1]

The tradition of musical patronage at Court was remarkably strong under all the Tudors. Indeed the establishment of Henry VIII included some seventy or eighty musicians. Inevitably the great households tried to emulate the Court. This tradition was perpetuated and even extended under Elizabeth. And if the landed nobles sometimes tried to ape their Continental (particularly Italian) counterparts it was only because they were endeavouring to show a natural regard for the progressive values of a civilised life. Their 'little kingdoms', in an age which was essentially rural, were extremely valuable in developing and sustaining all the qualities which the Renaissance had awakened. It is interesting to note that where a 'household did not retain plenty of musicians on its permanent staff, outside help was employed for special occasions. A troupe of players belonging to a nobleman would sometimes give its services to another mansion when its employer did not require it.'[2]

Apart from the aristocracy there was, too, an increasing 'upper-middle' class which shared in a good deal of the intellectual and artistic movements of the day. Merchants and yeomen, helped by the development of printing, were ready enough to imitate the cultural standards of their social superiors. Particularly because the Queen had 'lent a ready patronage to the new commerce; she considered its extension and protection as a part of public policy' and her statue in the centre of the London Exchange was a tribute of the great merchant companies to the interest with which she watched and shared personally in its enterprises. And from the grammar schools where music was an important subject in the curriculum would come many of the superior retainers and servants; for there is ample evidence to show that musical ability was an asset in seeking a place among the higher domestics of a household.

[1] *Short History of the English People*, J. R. Green (Macmillan), Vol. 2, p. 860 f.

[2] *Music and Poetry of the English Renaissance*, Bruce Pattison (Methuen), p. 4.

After the death of Elizabeth in 1603 and during the first two or three decades of the seventeenth century, the country was faced with growing complexities in religious, political, social and even industrial affairs. Nor must we forget the early visitation of the bubonic plague which troubled the land. Maurice Ashley in the second chapter of his *England in the 17th Century* (Pelican) offers an admirable summary of conditions and social changes which is quite illuminating. But the changes which were wrought in the social fabric had less influence on the progress of the English ayre, which will be our main concern here, than might have been expected. It is probable that the later years between the Civil War and the Restoration produced a more pointed change in the progress of the art generally.

Our survey of English song starts with the remarkable genius of William Byrd, the most distinguished musician of his age and certainly one of the greatest composers this country has ever known. Even though we are here concerned with only a small part of his work, his contribution to solo song, it will be enough to prove the truth of Fellowes's words: 'that among his many incursions into new fields not the least remarkable was that which led Byrd to become one of the earliest of all writers of *Lieder*'. There may be those who will look askance at the use of the word *Lieder*, implying that secular song would be more fitting; but not more accurate.

Undoubtedly the solo songs of Byrd stand apart from the general progress of the ayre. He wrote no accompaniments for the lute but always chose the consort of viols for this purpose. True, it is not always easy to decide whether a composition is for solo voice and strings or for unaccompanied voices because of the customary indication of the time that the music was 'apt for voices and viols'. But Byrd expressly tells us in his *Psalmes Sonets and Songs* (1588) that they were originally set for solo voice and strings and one could wish that some of them were more often heard in this form. The 'first singing part' is not always the soprano; for example, *Care for thy soul* and *Why do I use my paper* are alto solos. In the later *Psalmes Songs and Sonnets* (1611) the music is said to be 'framed to the life of the words' but also bears the familiar 'fit for Voyces or Viols'. This may seem to be somewhat haphazard but the performance of such music was essentially a private affair ready to use what resources were available at any particular time.

Fellowes is surely right in describing *My sweet little darling* as an 'exquisite little art-song'. It is now available in a modern issue by Stainer & Bell as is another equally attractive item *Ah silly soul*. Among other songs with string accompaniment must be listed *Oh that we woeful wretches*; *Methought of late in sleep*; and *How vain the toils*. Then there are the Christmas carol *From Virgin's Womb* and the New Year's Day carol *O God that guides the cheerful sun*, both for solo voice and chorus. And as an example of his originality in the field of dramatic song there is *Come tread the path* written as early as *c.* 1568 for a play *Tancred and Gismunda*.[1]

Similarly, solo songs with lute accompaniment were fairly normal in Europe from the middle of the century but though England was slow to take up the fashion, once she did so, she revealed a remarkable talent and skill as well as a striking poetic felicity. These ayres (one retains the old spelling for the sake of identity) were the work of a score of composers who flourished from 1597, the date of Dowland's first book, down to Attey's first book in 1622 or, possibly, down to the so-called *Madrigales and Ayres* by Walter Porter in 1632. All the composers were lutenists of high accomplishment. Dowland, indeed, had a wide Continental reputation, as well as his appointments to Lord Howard de Walden and James I. Daniel, Rosseter, Ferrabosco and Thomas Ford were likewise in Royal service. So, too, was Robert Jones, while Greaves was in the service of Sir Henry Pierrepoint. Not all were professional musicians in the narrow sense of that word. Pilkington was in Orders, a minor canon in Chester Cathedral, and Hume was an army captain. Campion was one of the greatest lyric writers of the age and a man of wide culture; a physician by profession and a distinguished poet by repute.

A cogent definition of the ayre has been provided by Bruce Pattison: 'The essence of the *Ayre* is the tune. Its distinction

[1] See also p. 1066, Vol. I, *Grove's Dictionary*, Fifth Edition, (Macmillan).

lies in its being the first English song in which the accompaniment is carefully composed yet purely subsidiary to the solo
voice. Strumming on an instrument to support the voice is as
old as instruments themselves; but there is nothing improvised
about the ayres. Their best composers were as technically
accomplished as the contemporary madrigal composers; they
just did not choose to employ their technique as Byrd had
employed his when he tried his hand at solo song. His song
melodies had been adapted to the requirements of the contrapuntal texture into which they were woven. The song melody,
on the other hand, *is* the air. The accompaniment is generally
harmonic, but even if it becomes contrapuntal, it is subordinate
to the solo part.'[1] Despite the fact that, as a concession to the
prevalent fondness for part-singing, many of the ayres were
described as for 'foure parts' and so on, it is plain that 'the
composer began with a tune'.

Thanks to the zeal of E. H. Fellowes and others, the repertoire of the lutenists is now readily available[2] and it behoves our
singers, both amateur and professional, to offer something
more than mere lip-service to a remarkable period in the history
of English song. Before singling out certain composers and
songs for particular mention, I would like to draw attention to
some stylistic features which should be apparent to the present-
day performer of the ayre. It was the late John Goss, I believe,
who once remarked that 'the English *Ayre* never forgets its
aristocratic upbringing'. He was referring principally to the
fact that the songs were originally written for performance
before a cultured and more or less private audience who could
appreciate technique and taste in both poetry and music.
True, the subsequent publication of the songs revealed a fairly
wide market for them—some were even circulated as broad-
sides—but though the ayre and the popular song of the period
might seem to have some things in common, the two forms are
distinct enough and the intrinsic artistry of the lutenists ought

[1] *Music and Poetry of the English Renaissance*, Bruce Pattison
(Methuen).
[2] *The English School of Lutenist Song writers*, ed. Fellowes (32 vols.),
Stainer & Bell. *English Ayres*, ed. Warlock & Wilson (6 vols.),
Oxford Press.

certainly to be preserved. This is not to say that the pursuit of refinement and elegance should minimise eloquence because many of the songs, even the simpler ones, are deeply-felt. Their performance should not be flamboyant or heavily vocalised but their lyrical nature should be maintained even for some of the more dramatic utterances. It must be remembered, too, that the original barring of the tune and the lute part was a guide for the eye and not in obedience to a time-signature, real or implied. When such barring is further edited in a more or less conventional way it must not be taken as suggesting a regular accent and so producing, at times, an arbitrary 'syncopation' which is not meant. The lutenist was acutely aware of the *proportions* of his music; he was more concerned with 'quantity' than with 'stress'; and he knew he could rely on singers to make 'little adjustments to compromise between the requirements of musical pattern and those of syllabic quantity'.[1]

Undoubtedly, the three greatest of the lutenists were Dowland, Daniel and Campion; though, perhaps, for different reasons. The well-known sonnet by Richard Barnfield though often attributed to Shakespeare which begins:

> If music and sweet poetry agree
> As they needs must the sister and the brother

specifically names Dowland and his 'heavenly touch upon the lute'. Apart from this he was an accomplished singer and probably a poet as well; and his musical genius, considerably enriched by his extensive travels on the Continent, is amply demonstrated in some eighty songs or more. His skill as a composer is surely unquestioned; and his vocal declamation is at once fluent and thoroughly effective. It has been said that he 'cared not a rap whether subsequent verses fitted the music so long as the first one hit the mark', but we may be reasonably sure that his own personal performance could surmount this difficulty with ease, and we might regret that he did not transcribe the required modifications. His range of expression

---

[1] Op. cit. Indeed, singers should study carefully Chapter VII of Bruce Pattison's book.

(Above) THOMAS TALLIS, *c.* 1505–1585
(Below) WILLIAM BYRD, 1543–1623

THOMAS LOWE, died 1783

KITTY CLIVE, 1711–1785

GEORGE FRIDIRIC HANDEL, 1685–1759
by Sir James Thornhill

THOMAS ARNE, 1710–1778

seems limitless. The direct merriment of *Fine knacks for ladies* (more often thought of and performed as a part-song nowadays); the buoyant gaiety of *Daphne*; the limpid rhythmic sweep of *Come again, sweet love doth now invite*; the manly tenderness of *Dear, if you change*; the skilful declamation of *Far from triumphing court* (published by his son Robert in *A Musical Banquet*); his folk-song felicity in *Now O now I needs must part*; and in *Can she excuse my wrongs* and *Shall I go walk the woods so wild* (where the melodic interest is so subtly transferred to the lute); the sheer pathos of *I saw my lady weep, Flow my tears* and *In darkness let me dwell*—these are but a few examples taken almost at random to avoid enumerating only my own particular favourites. One hopes they may suffice to incite singers to explore for themselves this 'mine of pure melody'.

John Daniel (sometimes spelt Danyel) in a score of *Songs for the lute, viol and voice* (1606) may not reveal the same wide range but of their skill and eloquence there can be no doubt. *Coy Daphne* is an example of the 'question and answer' song which was a fairly common device of the time; *Like as the Lute* and *Time cruel Time* are settings of distinguished poems by his elder brother Samuel; and his *Stay, cruel, Stay*; *Grief, keep within* and *Eyes look no more* are truly poignant examples of the 'pathetic' in song. There is often a marked originality in his bold chromaticisms, and in his use of vivid intervals and free rhythm to express all the emotional suggestions of the poetic text. And he can go beyond the strophic form to the *durchcomponirt* in song in his search for the faithful realisation of the poetry. Despite the slenderness of his output he must be counted among the greatest of English song-writers.

By contrast, the output of Thomas Campion (sometimes spelt Campian) runs to well over a hundred songs. In many ways he was a remarkably versatile man and the epitome of a poet-musician. He may not have had the overall skill and genius of Dowland nor the emotional depth of Daniel but he possessed a certain melodic felicity and the real sensitivity of a poet. He held rather positive opinions about matters like quantative metre and rhyme as well as the practical problems of setting poetry to music. His book, *Observations on the Art of English Poesie* (1602) is a highly individual theoretical study;

B

and his fame as an outstanding lyric poet is generally acknowledged. As a composer he would probably be deemed to be
something of a miniaturist although there is a distinctive charm
about all his music. Among the most familiar of his songs are
There is a garden in her face and *Never weather beaten sail* as well as
So sweet is thy discourse, Shall I come sweet love to thee and the
wistful *Oft have I sighed*. The aptness and freedom of his musical
phrasing is well demonstrated in songs like *Follow your saint,
My sweetest Lesbia* and *Love me or not*: while, for me at least,
among the more distinctive of his songs one would cite *Most
sweet and pleasing are Thy ways, The cypress curtain of the night* and
What if a day.

It is noteworthy that, unlike Dowland's, Campion's subsequent verses did fit the music as ably as the first verse which
prompts Wilfrid Mellers's suggestion that his method of working
was as a poet to write the first verse, then as a composer to set
the music before writing the subsequent verses. Thus, while
the music of the first verse was conditioned by the poetry, in the
subsequent verses the poetry was conditioned by the music.[1]

Campion's close friend and legatee, Philip Rosseter, has a
slighter musical talent but his *Though far from joy, And would
you see my mistress' face, If she forsake me, When Laura smiles,* and
Kind in unkindness might be cited as the best examples of his
work which was always thoroughly vocal and melodically
attractive. The song which has been acclaimed by Warlock, as
his masterpiece, *What then is love but mourning* is so short, a
mere ten bars, that I felt it was worth while to reproduce it in
full here.

Thomas Morley, whose fame rests more on his *Plaine and
Easie Introduction* (1597) as well as his canzonets and ballets and
some of his sacred music, was rather modest about his ability as
a 'professor' of lute ayres, but his fourteen songs *First Booke of
Ayres* (1600), now published under the editorship of Fellowes,
contains several attractive items in addition to the universally-
known *It was a lover*; even though he claims he was 'like a
blind man groping his way' who 'at length happened on a

---

[1] *Words and Music in Elizabethan England*, No. 2 Pelican Guide to
English Literature (Wilfrid Mellers).

What then is love but mourning

by Rosseter

What then is Love but mourn - ing? What de-sire but a self
Beau - ty is but a bloom - ing, Youth is his glo - ry en-
Sum-mer in Win - ter fa - - deth Gloom-y night heav'n-ly light

-burn - - ing? Till she that hates doth love re - turn
-tomb - - ing. Time hath a while which none can stay.
sha - - deth; Like to the morn are Ve - nus' flow'rs,

Thus will I mourn, Thus will I sing: Come a - way, come a-way, my dar - ling.
Then come away While thus I sing: Come a - way, come a-way, my dar - ling.
Such are her hours. Then will I sing: Come a - way, come a-way, my dar - ling.

method'. Thomas Ford is remembered chiefly for his *Since first I saw your face* more frequently sung now as an unaccompanied chorus; but the ten ayres from *Musicke of Sundry Kindes* (1607) are all well worth looking at particularly *Not full twelve years*. Ford may have 'conceived his airs as homophonic part songs', but Michael Cavendish, on the other hand, was more influenced by the madrigal. His best examples are *Love is not blind*; *The heart to rue* and *Down in a valley*. Robert Jones is a more lively and, in some ways, a more venturesome character. All his songs are eminently singable and generally cast in a simple mould. Many, indeed, have something of the artless charm of folk song and some possess some happily contrived rhythmic features. From his five sets of *Ayres* (1600, 1601, 1608, 1609 and 1610) one might cull the following as representative of his effective talent: *Now what is love*; *Go to bed sweet muse*; *Love is a pretty frenzy*; *The sea hath many thousand sands*; *Do not, O do not prize*; *My father would have me take*; *My complaining is but feigning*; *Love is a babel*; *Thinkest thou, Kate*, and *She hath an eye*. Francis Pilkington, for all his madrigalian style, is a thoroughly attractive composer who has some really graceful and polished songs; e.g., *Now peep, bo peep*; *With fragrant flowers* and *Rest sweet nymphs*.

The last named makes for a most interesting comparison with a twentieth-century setting of the same poem by Peter Warlock. Indeed, so many of the lutenists' poems, which are among some of the finest in a golden age of English lyric poetry, have attracted composers in later ages; and singers would find that a comparative study of them would teach them a good deal about the subtleties of vocal declamation. Similarly, among the lutenists themselves there are several settings of the same poem.[1] Not only does this provide an interesting comparison in matters of technique and style, it also cultivates a sensitive appreciation of the words themselves.

There are still a few composers to be considered. Ferrabosco, one of a family of Italian musicians who settled in England, was born in Greenwich in 1575. He was one of the King's Musicians under James I and had some reputation as a violist. He is best

---

[1] See *English Madrigal Verse*, E. H. Fellowes (Oxford), Part II.

known, perhaps, for his music to some of Ben Jonson's masques and earned a warm tribute from that poet as well as from Campion. From his book of *Ayres* (1609) *Come my Celia*; *O eyes, O mortal stars* and *Like hermit poor* could be named as characteristic examples. Cooper, who spent some of his early life in Italy, was inclined to spell his surname in the Italian way, Coprario. He was the music teacher for all the children of James I. From his first book (1606) probably *O sweet flower* is the best known; while from the second (1613), written in memory of Henry, Prince of Wales, to words by Campion, I would select *So parted you* as the most moving. Little is known about Corkine but from his two sets (1610 and 1612) one must name *Shall a frown*; *Sweet, let me go* and *Beauty sat bathing*. Peerson, whose accompaniments were set for three viols, expressly says they could also be for virginal or lute, the first mention in English music of the virginal to accompany the voice. His best songs, probably, are *O precious time*; *At her fair hands* and *Now, Robin, laugh and sing*. The songs of Tobias Hume, who was more of a mercenary soldier than a musician, are mainly of a convivial character. There is a sly humour in his *Tobacco* and a certain melodiousness in his *Fain would I change that note*. Bartlet's *Who doth behold* and *Whither runneth my sweetheart* as well as Greaves's *Flora; Celestina* and *Inconstant Laura* also call for honourable mention. One other composer who must be mentioned is Robert Johnson, who served under both James and Charles, and also taught Prince Henry. He was certainly an excellent lutenist and his songs often show a bold declamatory sense. Many of his theatre songs were published in contemporary anthologies. His best known are probably *Full fathom five, Where the bee sucks, Come charming sleep* and *Mine Host's song*, all of which, edited by Anthony Lewis, have been published by the Lyrebird Press.

It is hardly necessary to go through the entire list of the composers which ought to include the honourable name of Anonymous. All the songs are now fairly easily accessible for the reader's own scrutiny.[1] It must be said that the ayre at its

---

[1] Op. cit. See also Chapter XX, *English Madrigal Composers*, Fellowes (Oxford).

weakest sometimes betrays a certain quality of archness, with an over-reliance on sequential clichés, and even a dainty deliberateness of rhythm. But even among the more mediocre composers a few simple gems are to be found and there is no doubting the sheer English quality of them all.

A word must be said about a current fashion, which is growing, of singing the ayres to a guitar accompaniment. This may be appropriate enough, often more so than a stilted pianoforte accompaniment, but there are some important warnings. The *nature* of the originals must be preserved and needs something more than an elementary playing technique. Many of the more contrapuntal examples demand a skill approaching that of a Bream or a Gavall. Certainly there is no place for any indiscriminate strumming or vamping. The lutenists' accompaniments are too characteristic and important to be bowdlerised. And even when transferred, for convenience, to the piano, they will need always an expert and subtle realisation in tone and texture. Unfortunately, there are some editions of the lutenists' songs, on both sides of the Atlantic, in which the pianoforte realisations of the lute parts are both stylistically and harmonically inaccurate.

The prevalent notion that the ayres are only meant for men's voices needs examination. It is true that the musicians employed in Court and castle were nearly all men. It is equally true that a great many of the poems were the sentiments of 'any lover to his lady'. And there is a grain of truth in the statement that the *tessitura* of the male voice is more suited to the lute accompaniment. But the success which attended the first publications of the songs suggests that amateur singers were ready enough to avail themselves of the music; and there must have been some women singers among them. Moreover, many of the poems are as appropriate for women as for men and there are some which are surely eminently appropriate for women, to name Robert Jones's *Oh he is gone* or *Farewell fond Youth* as only two examples which spring almost unbidden to one's mind.

3

The Seventeenth Century

SOON after the death of Shakespeare in 1616 the musical
flame which had been kindled by the Tudors and nurtured
thereafter by the Elizabethans, began to show signs of burning
low. Not immediately so and it would be difficult to attribute it
to a single cause. The smouldering religious differences and the
political stresses were bound to have an unsettling effect though
nothing like the upheaval that was so soon to come. But, as
Blom has said: 'Musical life, at court as well as outside, went on
in the early years of the seventeenth century much as it had
done at the end of the sixteenth.'[1] The new impulse in music
in Italy, conveniently dated 1600, was not as revolutionary as it
is often represented; and its repercussions in England were
tardy and scarcely discernible for quite a time. A. K. Holland
has wisely reminded us: 'No artistic system is ever completely
and suddenly disrupted by the fulminations of a little group of
theorists';[2] any artistic developments must have time to grow.
That our native musical genius was waning is amply demonstrated by comparing, say, Dowland's first book with that of
Attey twenty-five years later. Even more so if one extends it
further to Walter Porter's *Madrigales and Ayres* (1632). Porter
was allegedly a pupil of Monteverdi, more certainly the Master
of the Choristers at Westminster Abbey and, for me at least, a
composer of limited ability. Even his exploitation of the Italian
device known as the *trillo*, the rhythmic re-iteration of notes,
was rather elementary. Purcell was to do it so much better and

[1] *Music in England*, Eric Blom (Pelican Books).
[2] *Henry Purcell*, A. K. Holland (Pelican Books).

for a more positive reason. The influence of the Italians in the matter of vocal declamation was destined to have a considerable influence on English song but the work of Porter scarcely serves as any bridge or link between the old and the new. There is later evidence and other considerations of more importance as we shall presently see.

Undoubtedly the spirit of the times was changing very rapidly. We need not follow too closely the historical ferment, whether in its religious, political, social or economic phases, although there must be some broad generalisations with which we will be concerned. Between James I and Charles I lies a period of constant turmoil; e.g., the tension between Parliament and the throne, the fluctuating balance of power in the social order, the first hint of an industrial revolution in the discovery that coal was a national asset, the holocaust of civil war, and the devastating visitations of the bubonic plague. There was a mood of revolution in the air even if it was but a vague shadow of the more fanatical French Revolution that was to darken the world more than a century later. Richard Law has asserted: 'The community has always counted for more than the State in England, and the individual for more than the community. The history of England, indeed, is the record of an endless campaign which the Englishman has waged to preserve or assert his liberties against a succession of tyrannies which threatened to overwhelm them. The Englishman made common cause with the Crown to curb the power of the barons or to limit the pretensions, when they seemed excessive, of the Church. He made common cause with Parliament, or with the great Lords of the revolution, to regulate and set limits to the authority of the Crown.'[1] But at the point we have here reached the voice of the people was hardly articulate above the noise of debate among their betters and the struggle for power among the privileged.

The cause of music was bound to suffer in the general discontent. Yet it managed to survive more or less, particularly in the popularity of the masque, until the Civil War and the power of the Puritans was in the ascendant. The bias of the latter may

---

[1] Chapter 2, *The Character of England*, ed. Barker (Oxford).

be less than is generally assumed but the effect of their ban is a matter of historical fact. Charles I, whatever he was as a monarch, was a connoisseur of the arts with the usual bias of royalty towards the foreign musicians. It is worth noting here that what Blom describes as the 'split between composition and performance as a musical avocation' was beginning to show. In a list of well over a hundred Court musicians named at the end of the reign of James I, only one is 'designated specifically as composer'. Which prompts one to mention the name of Arabella Hunt (*d.* 1705), a famous lutenist-singer of the times, but no composer. Both Purcell and Blow wrote songs for her and she was celebrated in poetry by Congreve.

Among the composers who flourished during the reign of Charles I, there are six who, for different reasons, have a bearing on the progress of English song; the Lawes brothers, John Wilson, Colman, Lanier and Matthew Locke. Henry Lawes, outliving his younger brother William, who was a casualty of the Civil War, had a considerable reputation in his day, earning poetic tributes from Milton and Herrick for his ability as a song writer and, indeed, as a singer. His original music to Milton's *Comus* is justly praised but his songs, for all their 'just note and accent' are somewhat insipid, too much subject to the bar-accent; and his rhythmic devices are sufficiently mechanical as to become monotonous. However, he has his importance as a transitional composer of vocal music at a time when the declamatory ideals of *Nuove Musiche* were slowly taking root. His taste is unquestioned but he lacks originality. Among the songs which have kept a place in the singer's repertoire are *Amarantha*; *I am confirmed a woman can*; *I prithee send me back my heart*; *Bid me but live*; *The angler's song* and the amusing *Tavola*, a satire on the Italian songs of the time, set to the Index of a book of Italian airs.[1] William Lawes was also much admired in his day and, in many ways, was a bolder composer than his brother. Singers know him chiefly nowadays by a solo arrangement of his part-song *Gather ye rosebuds*. He wrote the music (with Simon Ives) to Shirley's masque

---

[1] See also *Ten Ayres by Henry Lawes*, ed. Thurston Dart (Stainer & Bell).

B*

Triumph of Peace and also Davenant's *The Triumph of the Prince d'Amour*. His instrumental music is of real merit, and may have influenced Purcell.

The songs of John Wilson are pleasant and melodious; and the three best-known are *Take O take those lips away, Lawn as white as driven snow* and *In the merry month of May*. He was for a time Professor of Music at Oxford and it is certain he was much favoured by the King. His connection with the stage—he was thought to have taken the part of Balthazar who sings *Sigh no more ladies* in *Much Ado*[1]—is borne out by his close friendship with Alleyn the actor. Charles Colman (Coleman) and Nicholas Lanier are known mainly for the music they wrote for masques and other secular entertainments. Colman's daughter-in-law is said to have been one of the first women to appear on the English stage and Pepys has an interesting reference to her (October 1665): 'She sung very finely though her voice is decayed as to strength, but mighty sweet, though soft.' Lanier was also a painter of repute and spent some time in Italy as an agent of the King to buy pictures for the royal collection. Matthew Locke is more fittingly left to a later period for notice.

This may be an appropriate point to draw attention to the continued popularity of the masque and similar secular entertainments. Even the Puritans did not oppose them so long as they dealt with 'elevated subjects'. Blom's words are apposite. 'The English masque favoured the song as much as the dance, and it was here that composers found their widest scope in developing a type of declamatory or dramatic song that was akin to the later accompanied recitative in opera. There were formal, lyrical songs, too, corresponding to the later aria, though smaller and less highly organised. Settings, dresses and what would nowadays be called "production" were of the utmost importance—far more so than the music in fact, for had the composer's share in the work been at all comparable with that of the designer, or even with that of the "stage manager" the English early seventeenth-century masques would have grown unawares into full-dress operas similar to

---

[1] Nowadays it is thought that the Jacke Wilson was a boy who became a City wait and is not to be identified with the composer at all.

the most elaborate examples of baroque opera known to musical history—the Venetian opera of the second half of the century.'[1]

The actual publication of music during the reign of Charles I was disappointing as compared with the madrigalian and lutenist eras and had to await the advent of John Playford, whose *The English Dancing Master*, an important collection of folk tunes, appeared in 1651 and continued with fairly regular new editions far into the eighteenth century. The Puritans, strangely enough, offered no opposition to this. But in other ways, the Puritans' purge was disastrous for musicians. Between the execution of Stafford in 1641 and that of Charles eight years later we have to note that Hilton at St Margaret's, Porter and Portman at Westminster Abbey and Tomkins at Worcester were all dismissed; William Child was forced to retire and Christopher Gibbons, the son of Orlando, had to quit his post at Winchester while Rogers had to leave his post at Christ Church Cathedral in Dublin and take refuge as a lay-clerk at Windsor. Cromwell, as Lord Protector, was not above appropriating the organ at Magdalen College and installing it at Hampton Court where his daughters were taught to play by John Hingston. Some of the luckless musicians sought employment in the houses of the noble and wealthy, but the majority had to support themselves by teaching. Playford's list of London music teachers was of a despairing length and it is certain that many of them suffered utter poverty and want.

The population of England in the seventeenth century was less than a tenth of what it is today and about one-fifth of the total population was concentrated in what we now term the 'home counties'. The growth and importance of London was quite considerable and to some contemporaries was a matter of some concern. Bristol was the second largest port; and the cloth trade, then the principal industry, though organised on a loose domestic basis, brought no little significance to towns like Leeds, Norwich and York, while the increasing coal trade was bound to affect a town like Newcastle. Manchester and Birmingham were then little more than fair-sized villages.

---

[1] *Music in England*, Eric Blom (Pelican), p. 63.

Middlesex and Surrey were considered the richest counties, but the North of England was the poorest and a noted haunt for robbers and highwaymen. Dr Ashley has described the London of the time as the 'home of busy tradesmen and merchants, of poets and painters, of beautiful women and witty and intelligent men. Though it was a gay city, above all when decorated by the full pageantry of the Court, it was also incredibly dirty and smelly. Hackney and Stepney (which contained many French Protestant refugees) were overcrowded and insanitary, while modern suburbs, such as Kensington and Hampstead, were still country villages. When the frequent plagues or other reasons compelled the government and parliament to leave London, they usually met in Oxford, always a rallying point for Church and King, whereas Cambridge became the haunt of Puritans, Broad Churchmen, and Cromwellians.'[1]

It is not easy to bring the life and conditions of the first half of the seventeenth century into accurate focus in a few sentences. There are so many apparently contradictory impulses to be noted. G. M. Trevelyan is able to say that 'In the country at large the apprentice system, the poor law, the regulation of wages and prices, the economic and administrative functions of the Justices of the Peace under the control and stimulus of the Privy Council, were all much the same on the day when the Long Parliament met as on the day when Queen Elizabeth died'.[2] But a stern belief in witchcraft was rampant and the mania for the persecution of witches was at its highest point in the reign of James I. Yet Green could write that '. . . no greater moral change passed over a nation than passed over England during the years which parted the middle of the reign of Elizabeth from the meeting of the Long Parliament. England became the people of a book, and that book was the Bible.'[3] And it was religion as well as patriotic adventure which stimulated the 'beginning of the permanent expansion of the English race overseas' in the several emigrations to the New World and the trading stations on the coast of Hindustan.

[1] *England in the 17th Century*, Dr Maurice Ashley (Pelican), p. 13.
[2] *Illustrated English School History*, G. M. Trevelyan, Vol. 2 (Longmans, Pelican Books).
[3] Op. cit., Vol. 3, p. 935.

Meanwhile, the wanton creation of peerages and baronetcies by James I may have diluted the nobility but also provided opportunities for ambitious yeomen and enterprising professional men like lawyers and merchants to change their status and increase their influence on current affairs. But the Elizabethan image of 'milkmaids singing ballads' had a quaint echo in one of the charming love-letters of Dorothy Osborne written in 1653: 'I walk out into a common which lies hard by the house where a great many young wenches keep sheep and cows and sit in the shade singing of ballads.'

If rural England was comparatively untouched by the turmoil of the times, the greater villages and the growing townships were certainly bound to be more deeply involved and affected; by disease, the depressions of 1620 and 1640, and the simmering conflict which was destined to boil up into war. Perhaps the change that was taking place could be described as that of a nation moving, in all phases, religious, political, social and artistic, from the plains of medievalism to the foothills of modernity. Always remembering G. M. Trevelyan's wise reminder that while the 'Medieval idea of the supremacy of law as something separate from and independent of the will of the executive, disappeared in Continental countries . . . in England it became the palladium of our liberties and had a profound effect on English society and habits of thought'.[1] It must be remembered, too, that the Civil War was not a social rebellion but a struggle in which the community was divided on religious and political issues 'along a line of cleavage that answered, roughly and with many personal exceptions, to certain divisions of social type'.[2] So, as Winstanley averred, because it was not based on social revolution, its effects were bound to be negative, as the Restoration subsequently proved.

To the musicians, the prospect of the Restoration must have sounded a signal of hope. They were not to know, perhaps, that their salaries at Court thereafter were nearly always to be paid in arrears. They anticipated, no doubt a little ruefully, that a fresh influx of foreign musicians could be expected; but,

[1] Op. cit., p. 192.   [2] Op. cit., p. 187.

hopefully, they also thought the rapidly increasing public interest in the masque and similar entertainments as well as the removal of the tiresome Puritan restrictions of their art, would increase their prospects. Moreover, once the Civil Wars were over, there was a distinct revival of economic prosperity with less restrictions on trade and on labour. Everything seemed set for happier times. They were not to know that on the very eve of the Restoration, so to speak, the world depression of 1659 would confront the new king with serious difficulties. Perhaps all that they were most interested in was the return of the monarchy itself, for the monarchy is an institution the Englishman has always cherished. This was the England into which Henry Purcell, perhaps our greatest musical genius, was born.

There is no necessity for me to be much concerned here with biographical detail. There are at least three outstanding biographies already to hand.[1] Sir Jack Westrup, whose cool judgement and cogent information cannot conceal his warm affection for his subject, has produced a complete biography which is hardly likely to be surpassed. Dennis Arundell, perhaps slightly but engagingly influenced by his theatrical expertise, offers a thoroughly stimulating essay; while A. K. Holland, in his forthright and racy style of lively prose, reveals all the animation and excitement of the real enthusiast. All three bear testimony to the attractive personality of the composer who, in his short lifetime, was generally acknowledged as a Master. The concluding paragraph of Westrup's book is a superb encomium. 'Judgements of Purcell's art have differed according to individual reactions. Some have found it feminine and yielding, others have been struck by its boisterous energy. In art as in religion, we are apt to discover what we hope to find, to judge the source by the extent to which it supplies our own thirst. What no-one will fail to find in Purcell at his best is a spring of life, a vitality which glows with the effort of the whole man. To listen is to share an experience, to catch some of his glancing fire and to have a part in his aching regret. He was a man of changing moods and sympathies, ready to boast, to

---

[1] *Purcell*, J. A. Westrup (Dent); *Henry Purcell*, Dennis Arundell (Oxford); *Henry Purcell*, A. K. Holland (Penguin).

worship, to sigh and to lament. He could bid the trumpets sound for majesty, or seeking flight from love's sickness find the fever in himself.'

It may seem scarcely necessary to underline the great importance of Purcell in the history of English song. Not infrequently, however, English singers are inclined to treat his songs as period pieces; and by confining their attention only to some of the established favourites, they miss something of the versatility of his vocal music and its technical importance in the sheer development of the singer's art. Being a singer himself, Purcell understood the human voice as few English composers have done, and 'though he makes considerable demands on his singers, they are never unreasonable'.[1] The English singer whose teaching does not include a reasonably detailed study of Purcell is only half-trained. Not that singers and singing teachers are wholly to blame. The modern publications of Purcell's songs are somewhat haphazard. A certain number of small volumes are available[2] and there are numerous single items to be found among the sheet-music issues of many publishers, though not all of them are authentic. But if some philanthropist could be found who would finance the publication of a comprehensive set of uniform volumes of the songs at a reasonably modest price, it could be of inestimable value to our native singers and students, both amateur and professional; and it would be a fitting tribute to a musical genius who, although silenced by death when Bach and Handel were only ten years of age, has surely revealed that 'his view of music was identical with that of the modern musician'.[3]

[1] *Purcell and the Singer's Art*, Norman Platt. Festival of Britain (1951) concert programme, ed. Watkins Shaw (Arts Council).

[2] For example Novello publish a set of seventeen songs ed. Somervell as well as two sets of fifteen. Albums of *Six Songs* ed. Moffatt are published by Forsyth Bros. and also by Bayley and Ferguson. An album of *Nine Songs* ed. Tippett and Bergmann published by Schott is important and the Purcell albums ed. by Britten & Pears although regarded by some as carrying their modernisation beyond the claims of editing should also be consulted.

[3] *Grove's Dictionary*, Vol. VI, p. 1009.

Such a venture would call for careful selection and, perhaps, some kind of appropriate categorisation; as well as a scrupulous editorship, particularly in the 'realisation' of the accompaniments, without too much over-elaboration of the inner parts which the composer probably never intended, and, of course, in the matter of transposition to suit the modern voice. Purcell's predilection for the counter-tenor voice and for some of the virtuoso singers of his day may present some problems which, however, are not impossible to overcome. And who knows, perhaps our singers, faced with some of Purcell's demands, might learn to get nearer the achievements of a golden age in singing.

Before passing on to a general discussion of Purcell's songs, we must notice the work of Matthew Locke, whose asperity often matched his considerable musical genius. Undoubtedly he was 'one of the strongest influences on English music of the Restoration period'.[1] His close friendship with the Purcell family is well known and is eloquently demonstrated by Purcell's own *Elegy on the death of his Worthy Friend, Mr Matthew Locke*, which was published in the second volume of Playford's *Choice Ayres* (1679) two years after Locke's death. That he was a man of very strong opinions is easily demonstrated but it is a pity that so much has been made of his acrimonious nature. His claim for his music to Shadwell's *Psyche* as 'An English Opera' is not so extravagant as it seems because the preface to his instrumental music to Shadwell's version of *The Tempest* a year later (1674) showed that he held positive and practical views about the proper form for opera. That he had absorbed much from the examples of the French stage and had fused them with the traditions of the English masque is self-evident. In the same way, his confidence in his declamatory song writing showed his ability to apply the current Italian principles to his native tongue.[2] Two other examples of his enterprise can be seen in a Curtain tune to the *Tempest* which may be regarded as one of the earliest storm fantasies of programme music; and his *Melothesia*, a short treatise on playing 'upon a Continued Bass'

[1] *Grove's Dictionary*, Vol. V, p. 354.

[2] *Three songs of Matthew Lock*, ed. Anthony Lewis (Lyrebird Press).

is generally considered to be the first English publication of its kind.

'Music is the exaltation of poetry. Both of them exist apart, but they are most excellent when they are joined.' These are Purcell's own words, even if Dryden wrote them, and he certainly lived up to them.[1] Even when the poetry he was dealing with was somewhat mediocre and, perhaps, rather futile. The 'spine' of his immortal melodies is the perfection and sheer spontaneity of his English declamation. Indeed it is an oft-repeated remark that even in his instrumental music 'he speaks English'. True as this may be, it must be accepted as a narrow concept of his skill. He was, above all, a distinctly professional composer who had absorbed all the current influences and developments of his day to invest them with his own individual style. His confident genius could look back and forwards with equal assurance and success. I have long cherished a secret belief that Purcell, Mozart and Schubert, were the three most *instinctive* composers in the whole history of the art. They are certainly the supreme melodists. And all three were short-lived, as though the originality and inventiveness of their musical minds could not suffer too long the vagaries of this somewhat hapless planet.

With something like three hundred songs to contemplate, apart from the solo cantatas, sacred solos, duets and so on, an adequate review of Purcell's vocal output is clearly impossible here. Even to analyse the important stylistic features of his versatile genius would be fairly extensive and would demand numerous musical quotations. A few salient points, however, must concern us. Purcell's song-forms are always organic and never founded on mere symmetry. Professor Dent's masterly analysis of *When I have often heard (Fairy Queen)*[2] is a striking example. The simple rondo form of *I attempt from Love's sickness (Indian Queen)* is so apt that any edition with interpolated pianoforte *ritornelli* is utterly inexcusable, especially for what Westrup has rightly described as 'the most perfectly poised melody

---

[1] This is a reasonable assumption, even though Dryden wrote the dedication to *Dioclesian* for Purcell.

[2] *Music & Letters*, October 1936, pp. 317–18.

Purcell ever wrote'.[1] There is, too, the rondo aria *Lucinda is bewitching fair* (*Abdelazar*) which deserves to be better known than it is. His masterly use of a ground bass is well known and is amply demonstrated in *When I am laid in earth* (*Dido and Aeneas*), the 'evening hymn' *Now that the sun* and *Music for awhile* (*Oedipus*), to name but three. Sometimes these ground basses are built on phrase lengths of five bars, 'and the superior parts by no means always coincide with these divisions'.[2] Notice, too, how in *Ah Belinda* (*Dido and Aeneas*), the voice anticipates the ground bass at the words 'Peace and I are strangers grown' and then ends with an expressive extension to five bars. Purcell had a particular liking for irregular patterns and free phrasing. For example, in *Cease O my sad soul* he divides a fifteen-bar group into seven, five and three: and the apparent four-bar phrase of *Come unto these yellow sands* consists of three and one.

It has long been established that Purcell's recitatives must be sung in strict time. Much the same could be said about all his songs. His immaculate vocal declamation is not helped by fanciful or forced idiosyncrasies in rhythmic interpretation. Tempo, too, will always depend on the appropriate expression and inflexion of the words. For example, the concluding section of *Ye twice ten hundred deities* (*Indian Queen*) is often sung faster than the dreamy tranquility of the text suggests. The 'mad songs' with their vivid changes of tempo, like *Bess O'Bedlam*, have an intrinsic sense of musical proportion if governed by the expressive needs of the text. All his songs of this genre, based on the contemporary attitude towards madness, are really effective, e.g., *I'll sail upon the dog-star* (*A Fool's Preferment*), *Let the dreadful engines* (*Don Quixote*, i) and *From Rosy Bowers* (*Don Quixote*, iii), the last named being known as 'the last song that Mr Purcell sett, it being in his sickness'. The confident range of his vocal *bravura* is really evident in his many dramatic arias. The most famous is *Arise ye subterranean winds* (*The Tempest*) and Westrup's comparison of Reggio's setting of these words with Purcell's[3] reveals how far Purcell had outdistanced his contemporaries.

[1] Op. cit., p. 84.
[2] A. K. Holland, op. cit., p. 101.
[3] Op. cit., p. 146.

One must acknowledge that the doubts which have arisen about the authorship of the music for the 1695 *Tempest* question Purcell's authorship of this magnificent song. The whole controversy has been amply discussed in Margaret Laurie's paper to the Royal Music Association[1] and also in Robert Etheridge Moore's *Henry Purcell and the Restoration Theatre* (Heinemann) Chapter VII, but I find myself coming down on the side of the latter who asserts roundly that the '*Tempest* is predominantly Purcell's'. Like Sir Jack Westrup I would ask, if not by Purcell, then by whom? Not Weldon, even if Miss Laurie's assertion that the figuration of his '*Destracted I turn* is similar to parts of *Arise ye Subterranean winds*' is accepted. See also *While these pass o'er the deep*, also from *The Tempest*. Purcell's abundant technique and a sure singer's instinct enable him to range with equal fidelity from the delicate *Still I'm wishing* (*Dioclesian*) and the simple charm of *The Knotting Song* to the deeply moving *The fatal hour* or the free and florid declamation of the remarkable *Not all my torments*: or from the spirited flexibility of the *coloratura* arias of the *Fairy Queen*, *Hark how all things* and *Hark the echoing air* to the sensitive detail of *Tell me some pitying angel*, also known as the Blessed Virgin's expostulation, and the recently discovered Meditation, *It must be done O my soul*: or from the simple animation of *How blest are shepherds* (*King Arthur*) and *What shall I do to show how much I love her* (*Dioclesian*) to the unhurried *sostenuto* of *If music be the food of love* (first and second settings) and the graphic chromaticism of *Next Winter comes slowly* (*Fairy Queen*).

The fact that school children are quite familiar with songs like *Fairest Isle* (*King Arthur*) and *Nymphs and Shepherds* (*The Libertine*) should not blind us to their technical qualities. In the former, his characteristic triple-time measure, which seems so suited to the stresses of English poetry, is not a mere formal device; the melody soars easily and spontaneously over the chains of the bar line for fluent and widely-ranging phrases. The natural melodic buoyancy of the second song is quite irresistible and yet, note how the melodic sweep is arrested at the words 'sacred to ease . . .' to be followed soon afterwards by

---

[1] *Proc. Royal Mus. Ass.*, Vol. 90 (1963–64), p. 43.

the rippling roulade on 'dancing'. Still the music sounds as inevitable as life. This ability for vivid word-painting is often made the occasion for powerful roulades which are far more than vocal embellishments; or some irregular resolved suspensions, as in *What can we poor females do?* as well as in the change of mood in *Anacreon's defeat* from the humorous beginning to the serious ending on 'he dies'. Similarly, his repetition of comparatively unimportant words, like 'all, all' or 'thus, thus', etc., are not the naïve devices they may seem; they have a dramatic significance in vocal expression. On his disconcerting traits in harmonic progression, often startling and so modern, Dr Whittaker's essay, 'Some observations on Purcell's harmony', is well worth study.[1]

Dr Ernest Walker, understandably enough, considered that English music at the end of the seventeenth century 'was an artistic cul-de-sac'. The remark, perhaps, might be applied more forcibly to the end of the next century, but it must be acknowledged that Purcell's younger contemporaries were of much less stature than their elders. The slender talents of John Eccles were mainly devoted to stage music but some of his songs (in 1710 he published a collection of nearly a hundred) still keep a place in the repertoire, e.g., *Fair Amoret, The jolly jolly breeze, The Avowal*. By contrast, John Weldon's ability was more significant, as one might have expected from an actual pupil of Purcell's. Although his reputation nowadays rests mainly on his church music, his music for the stage was quite admirable and from his songs, three books of which were published, at least two, *From Grave lessons* and *The Wakeful nightingale* are still sung today. And three songs by Daniel Purcell, *Lovely charmer, Let not love on me bestow* and *Cupid make your virgins tender* must be mentioned here as must some of the songs written by the well-known singer of the time, Richard Leveridge, even though he is now best known only as the composer of *The roast beef of old England*. There is still a place for his *Black-eyed Susan, When dull care, The sweet rosy morning, The Beggar's Song* but, perhaps, his most appealing songs are *Send back my long-strayed eyes to me* and *Sweet are the charms of her I love*.

[1] *Collected Essays*, W. G. Whittaker (Oxford).

Towards the end of the century, the introduction of engraving cheapened the publication of sheet music and the market became flooded with 'anthologies' of songs, written, principally, for the stage, the concert and the singing teacher. The widespread success of these publications, though they were somewhat inaccurate and mixed in quality, revealed the popularity of singing at the time. Indeed, there is ample evidence of some excellent singing teaching stemming probably from the restoration of the Chapel Royal, and the practical influence of Henry Cooke, who was described by Evelyn in his *Diary* (28 October 1654) as 'the best singer' after the Italian manner in England. As Henry Cooke's pupils included most of the leading musicians of the day, this influence was bound to be extensive. Moreover, the establishment of Banister's Concert Room in Whitefriars in 1672 was soon followed by five others running in the metropolis, and in addition 'music began to be provided more liberally in taverns; all this shows that music was appealing to a much wider circle', but as we shall see, this had its perils as well as its potential.

4

The Eighteenth Century

THE eighteenth century witnessed an outstanding growth in
English commerce and finance and, indeed, in the early
foundations of the British Empire. Even the war with France
after 1689 failed to halt the general prosperity; nor did the
other conflicts of the time. The standard of living throughout
the country gradually rose from 1688 onwards and all classes
benefited from the improved trading conditions which developed with increasing liveliness from the Restoration
onwards. It was in 1718 that William Wood, a secretary to the
Customs, was able to report: 'From the year 1688 to this time,
we have gone on *increasing* our stock, notwithstanding the many
convulsions the Nation has had in respect of its *Trade* abroad
and *Credit* at home.' Inevitably this brought a new distinction to
the mercantile classes and it was the Whig journalist, Richard
Steele, who wrote in October 1713: 'All other subjects of our
Island from the highest to the lowest are as much below the
Merchant in political merit as that ravenous worm in the
entrails of the State, the stock jobber.' But the Parliamentary
Act of 1697 which was intended to curb unscrupulous speculation more or less established stockbroking as an honourable
profession, and so 'The pursuit of wealth as an end in itself
became a respectable calling'.[1] As witness the career of James
Brydges, the first Duke of Chandos. 'Patron of architects and a
generous sponsor of musical performance,' Brydges improved
upon his position in the Government service (he was at one
time Paymaster General) by judicious investment at a time

[1] *A Social History of English Music*, E. D. Mackerress (Routledge).

when innumerable projectors were busily forming new companies in an attempt to profit from the expanding market. Few of his contemporaries were able to survive the South Sea *debacle* as did the Duke of Chandos, yet Brydges's aspirations— so typical of that age—were shared by dozens of lesser men who could not possibly lay claim to his abundant riches.[1] This brings us directly to the career of Handel to whom the Duke was a most generous patron and at an important point in the progress of English music. From 1717 to 1720 when no Italian operas were given in London, Handel lived at the country seat of the Duke near Edgware and it was here, so to speak, that the English oratorio was born, inasmuch as the masque *Esther* which he wrote here was destined to become his first oratorio. Probably the motive which brought Handel to England was much the same as that which had prompted the influx of foreign musicians from the Restoration onwards, but it is also reasonably certain that many English aristocrats who had witnessed the composer's triumphs in Europe, particularly in Venice where his *Agrippina* had been an outstanding success, had added their persuasions with promises of active support when he did arrive. At all events, it must be acknowledged that without the aid of Handel's genius, Italian opera in England might have failed dismally because, prior to his advent, its hold on the public was rather precarious[2] and had been the subject of much derisive comment including Dr Johnson's famous remark when he described it as 'an exotic and irrational entertainment which has always been combated and has always prevailed'. As Dr Ernest Walker has said: 'It was exotic because it was strangely believed that no other language was admissible for artistic opera; and it was irrational because the composer's own designs were fettered at every turn by the necessity of conciliating the singers. The musical world has never seen a race of men and women whose outlook was so entirely bounded by the horizon of their own little vanities: solo singers have indeed been as a rule, up to a time that is within living memory, artistically the lowest class of musicians,

---

[1] Op. cit.
[2] *The Critic at the Opera*, Dennis Arundell (Benn).

but the full-blown tyrannously selfish conceit of the *prima donna*
and *primo uomo* of Handel's day was something unique. On pain
of a displeasure which would have wrecked the whole concern,
the composer had continually to be writing his music round the
particular voices of Cuzzoni or Faustina, Caffarelli or Farinelli,
affording frequent and varied opportunities for personal
display, minimising mutual jealousies, and consequently letting
the organic features of his work take care of themselves;
opportunities for anything like dramatic characterisation were
few and far between and the net result was a collection of
stereotyped airs strung together by the slenderest threads . . . the
entertainment was simply a concert with scenery and costume
in which singers competed strenuously with each other for the
favours of the arbiters of taste and fashion.'[1] The notorious
public quarrel of Signora Margarita de l'Epine and Mrs Tofts
in 1704 was one of the earlier manifestations of this deplorable
and incredible jealousy.

To the present generation Handel's Italian operas are little
more than names, except for a number of arias which have been
published separately some, unfortunately, to English words
which bear little or no resemblance to the mood or meaning of
the original text. Some of Handel's finest vocal writing is seen in
these operatic arias and since they were written for singers
who, for all their pettiness, were possessed of a remarkable
vocal technique, they should be of particular significance for
singers and singing teachers. In the earlier editions of *A History
of Music in England*, Dr Ernest Walker set forth a selected list of
some thirty-six titles which subsequently formed the basis of a
Handel edition by Dr Whittaker.[2] This list was omitted from
the later edition, probably because of Whittaker's work, but it
seemed to me worth while to reprint it here in an appendix
(Appendix B, page 147) for easy reference by singers and
teachers.

It may seem somewhat irrelevant to pursue so far a discussion of Handel's operatic work in an essay concerned with
English song but there are some important reasons for doing so.

---

[1] *A History of Music in England* (2nd Edition), Ernest Walker.
[2] Oxford University Press.

Handel's vocal writing generally was a notable influence on the development of singing technique and, although his influence on English music was more directly through oratorio than opera, we cannot forget that the modern oratorio had 'its artistic birth in Italy simultaneously with opera'. True, the Handelian oratorio is something *sui generis* because the composer had a particular genius for adaptation to his environment. Apart from the *Messiah*, which is unique, it was as much an entertainment as the opera was: 'sometimes consisting, like *Solomon* and *Israel in Egypt*, chiefly of imposing choruses, sometimes like *Joseph* and *Jephtha* of a judicious blend of biblical history and a decorous "love-interest", sometimes again, of vivid drama like *Saul* and *Belshazzar*; but compared with Schütz and Bach, it is always of "the earth, earthy" and the choral utterance is not so much the sentiment of the actors in the story, but more frequently the reflection of the religiously-minded listener'.[1]

Clearly, Handel never intended the oratorio as a devotional exercise as the early theatre performances prove. His motives were abundantly clear and practical. Faced with the recession in operatic interest in the late 1720s and the striking success of *The Beggar's Opera* in 1728, he turned towards this new activity, like the opportunist he was, because he saw in it a chance to recoup his operatic losses and he probably felt, instinctively, that it suited the native temperament. The acclaim for *The Beggar's Opera* was not as unanimous as it might seem. Indeed, Thomas Herring, subsequently Archbishop of Canterbury, preached a sermon against it in Lincoln's Inn Chapel: 'It has, I think, been generally agreed among moralists that all public entertainments should be so regulated as to have a tendency to the encouragement of virtue and the discountenancing of vice and immorality.' And it was Defoe, speaking of the contemporary underworld, who wrote: 'Thieves are set out in so amiable a light in *The Beggar's Opera* that it has taught them to value themselves on their profession rather than be ashamed of it, by making a highwayman the hero and dismissing him at last unpunished.' It may have been some of the same moralists

---

[1] *Grove's Dictionary of Music and Musicians*, Vol. VI, p. 254.

who at first questioned the propriety of performing oratorio in the theatre, though this opposition was shortlived and oratorio was accepted as a fitting and laudable complement to formal worship. For the earlier productions Handel still employed Italian singers, but he soon turned to native singers, whom he found far less expensive, and more amenable to his own teaching. 'For a number of years Handel worked concurrently on both operas and oratorios and in some cases there is not much to choose between the style of composition used for each.'[1] This is not to say that his approach to an operatic text was the same as to a religious one. Handel never wore his piety on his sleeve and the affirmations of an important tenet in the Christian faith in arias like *I know that my Redeemer liveth* and *The trumpet shall sound* reveal an emotion which is quite profound; and he could effect the ineffable simplicity and comfort of *Come unto Him* by using the melody (or part of it) of a Neapolitan carol[2]— a *canzone dei zampognati*—which he had heard in Naples in 1708, and had used subsequently for a set of variations. It is interesting to note that some of Handel's most inspired music is to be found in the non-religious works, like *Acis and Galatea* and *Semele*, and from the latter comes the singularly beautiful *O Sleep why dost thou leave me*, one of his finest compositions which, unfortunately, has suffered from some thoughtless editing in more recent issues. The rest of Handel's choral works also have many points of interest for singers and an edition of arias therefrom edited by Ford and Erlebach[3] is eminently worth scrutiny. So, too, are the nine religious arias to words by Heinrich Brockes.[4]

It is important to remember that Handel was writing during a 'period when the art of singing became epitomised into a style and technique that set the model for correct singing throughout the Western world. This era was that of the so-called *bel canto*, a term now generally used to denote that

[1] *Social History of English Music*, E. D. Mackerress, p. 99.

[2] *Clarendon Book 2 of Christmas Carols & Songs*, Wiseman & Northcote (Oxford Press), p. 32.

[3] In six vols.: (i) Dramatic Soprano; (ii) Lyric Soprano; (iii) Contralto; (iv) Tenor; (v) Bass (Boosey & Hawkes).

[4] Edited by Dr Roth (Brietkopf & Hartel).

flowering of vocal lyricism which reached its peak during the course of the eighteenth century.'[1] Unfortunately, the term *bel canto* is now very carelessly used, often being little more than sheer 'studio cant'. To quote Duey again: 'The term *bel canto* does not appear as such during the period with which it is most often associated, i.e., the seventeenth and eighteenth centuries: this may be said with finality. The popular conception that the teaching methods of the *bel canto* were secret and have been lost is proven a myth. Too many teachers have trafficked thus, albeit claiming at the same time to possess the secret themselves. Quite to the contrary, the methods appear to be so obvious, easy and natural. All that is needed is the light of musicological investigation in each aspect [which will reveal] an amazingly direct and simple approach to the business of singing. It must be admitted that the particular vocal technique and virtuosity of the *bel canto* may be impossible to achieve today. The particularly singular and unnatural gifts of the *castrati* due to a bizarre custom, now uncountenanced for the purpose of the art of song, lifted vocalism to an apogee no longer within the realm of probability; but their twin ideals of beautiful tone and florid line are still highly desirable in performance, and when achieved in substantial measure, are greatly enjoyed [and] the vocal masterpieces of the seventeenth and eighteenth centuries will not reveal their true worth except when performed with the lyrical and florid qualities of *bel canto*.'[2] Something of this concern for tone and sheer flexibility may be seen in a peculiar way in the success of a small choral group of today, the Swingle Singers, who sing examples of Bach's instrumental music with a remarkable skill in vocal flexibility and a subtle use of 'vocables' to obtain the requisite tone quality; so producing a vocalism which can render all the expressive qualities of instrumental music without the use of words.

We must be careful not to pursue this topic too far, lest we get involved in a discussion of singing teaching which will engender more heat than light. A comment by Mollie Sands is apposite. Speaking of the pleasure gardens of London, she says: 'Yet the

[1] *Bel Canto in its Golden Age*, P. A. Duey (Columbia University Press).
[2] Op. cit., pp. 11 and 155.

bel canto lived in the public taste in spite of the ridicule poured upon its exaggerations and the two kinds of singing—Italian and English—soon settled down and lived together peaceably. Some singers successfully practised both.'[1] And if we agree with the generally accepted view that the apotheosis of the *bel canto* style is reached in Rossini and Mozart,[2] there is some significance in the fact that two British singers of the time 'created' principal parts in the first performance of *Figaro* in Vienna in 1786, Michael Kelly as Basilio and Curzio, and Nancy Storace as Susanna.

Here we might digress for a moment to introduce Johann Christophe Schmidt of Ansbach, a friend of Handel's who early on had joined him in London to be his treasurer and act as agent for his music. The oft-repeated legends about Handel's bankruptcies have already been discountenanced by Dr Percy Young.[3] It now seems clear that he had several friends in financial circles, and he was able to recoup his heavy losses by prudent investment.[4] Schmidt's son of the same name, but anglicised to John Christopher Smith, revealed an early aptitude for music and after being taught by Handel, Pepusch and Roseingrave, attained to a certain recognition in English musical circles. In 1754 he was appointed organist of the Foundling School Chapel and in the same year he had a distinct success with an opera *The Fairies* (adapted from *Midsummer Night's Dream*). Two years later came his opera *The Tempest*, again adapted from Shakespeare, which contained two songs, *Full Fathom Five* and *The Owl is abroad*, which became long established popular favourites. Indeed, the second was mistakenly attributed to Purcell. But how a setting of words by Ben Jonson gets into *The Tempest* is not so easy to explain. When Handel's sight began to fail, it was Smith who acted as his amanuensis, and when the composer died he bequeathed

---

[1] *Invitation to Ranelagh*, Mollie Sands (John Westhouse), p. 27.

[2] *An essay on Bel canto*, Herman Klein (Oxford Press).

[3] 'Handel the Man', Percy M. Young, in *Handel: A Symposium*, ed. Gerald Braham.

[4] *Judas Maccabeus* and *Alexander Balus* were specially written to please the Jews who had aided Handel in his financial difficulties in 1745.

his original MS scores to him. These Smith subsequently presented to George III, and they are now in the King's Music Room at the British Museum.

The three most important English contemporaries of Handel were Dr William Croft, Dr William Boyce and Dr Thomas Augustine Arne. Dr Croft's musical reputation rests securely on his excellent church music, while Boyce's greatest contribution also concerns church music, in his compiling and editing of the three-volume *Cathedral Music*, despite his doubtful treatment of the Purcell items. Boyce seems to have been a lovable character, being particularly kind and helpful to younger musicians. As a composer he was hardly inferior to Arne, with whom he was often associated in works for the stage and the pleasure gardens for which they wrote many songs. Two quite successful stage productions of his were *Peleus and Thetis* (1747) and *The Chaplet* (1749). An attractive serenata *Solomon* (1743) includes a long-popular tenor solo *Softly rise O Summer breeze* (with bassoon obbligato) as well as the charming *Tell me lovely shepherd* and *Balmy sweetness ever flowing*.[1] *Heart of Oak*, the song by which Boyce is universally known, was first sung by Champness, the bass, in *Harlequin's Invasion*, a pantomime by Garrick which is now completely forgotten. Other songs by Boyce which have held a place in the vocal repertoire are *Tho' Chloe's out of fashion*[2] (one of John Beard's favourite items at Ranelagh), *Tell me no more I am deceived*, *The Song of Momus to Mars* (from Dryden's *Secular Masque*),[3] *On a bank beside a willow*,[4] *Colin's Success*[4] and *O fie Shepherd fie*.[4] More and more people are now discovering that Boyce is not to be easily dismissed as a very minor composer, because as more of his music comes to light, particularly the instrumental items, Burney's opinion of him seems fully justified. 'There is an original and sterling merit in his productions that gives to all his works a peculiar stamp and character of his own.'[5] He was created a Doctor of Music at Cambridge University in 1749.

[1] Edited Eric Taylor (Oxford Press).
[2] See *Five Songs*, arr. Mullinar (Augener).
[3] Edited G. P. Arkwright (Oxford Press).
[4] Edited Elizabeth Poston (Curwen).
[5] *Grove's Dictionary*, Vol. I, p. 863.

Thomas Augustine Arne, like Boyce, was born in 1710, the year of Handel's first arrival in England; and if he is not a truly great composer he is certainly, in Julian Herbage's words, 'a highly individual and accomplished one'.[1] There were unfortunate traits in his character which repelled rather than attracted friends. It is difficult to excuse his cruelty to his wife, the singer, Cecilia Young, whom he married in 1737. 'He seems to have been a flagrantly unfaithful husband and to have aroused much indignation by treating her with a cruelty that was said to go much beyond mere infidelity.'[2] They were not reconciled until 1777, the last year of the composer's life. He died in March 1778, but neither these facts nor the biased opinions of Dr Burney should colour our evaluation of Arne, the composer. When in 1738 he was commissioned to write the music for Dalton's adaptation of Milton's *Comus* for Drury Lane, Arne produced a near-masterpiece. As Herbage has said: 'From the bacchanalian tenor opening: *Now Phoebus sinketh in the West* to the graceful miniature cantata *How gentle was my Damon's air*,[3] every pleasurable emotion is expressed in a stream of natural, easy and, above all, elegant melody including the much-loved *Would you taste the noontide air?*' The work has now been reprinted in the *Musica Britannica* series. Arne's setting of Congreve's masque *The Judgment of Paris* also contains much fine music, including the songs in which the three goddesses compete for the golden apple and the better known tenor aria, *O ravishing delight*, nowadays appropriated for the soprano repertoire. This song is typical of Arne's expressive lyricism. Any intensely dramatic rendering hardly does it justice. Intrinsically it calls for ecstatic rather than an excited expression and the *Allegro* movements should be vivacious rather than fast. It is a pity that the recitatives and choruses of this work have been lost because it is a dramatic work which lends itself to present-day performance. I remember taking part in a private performance by students in Oxford nearly fifty years ago and greatly enjoying it. I have not been able to trace any performances other than the first in Cliveden 1740, in

[1] *Proc. Royal Mus. Ass.*, Vol. 78, 1951–2, p. 83 f.
[2] *Grove's Dictionary*, Vol. I, p. 209.
[3] Now re-issued under the doubtful title of *The Maiden's Lament*.

Dublin 1744 and Drury Lane 1745. Herbage thinks that Handel's *Semele* may have been influenced by this work of Arne's.[1] Another famous work by Arne is, of course, the masque *Alfred* by Thomson and Mallet (1740), of which the finale includes the famous *Rule Britannia* which everyone knows; but far too few know the excellent opening song *O Peace thou fairest child of heaven* or *If those who live in Shepherd's bower*[2] or *Come calm content*.[3]

The Shakespeare songs for which Arne is, perhaps, best known, start with the revival of *As you like it* at Drury Lane in 1740. In this two celebrated singers, Kitty Clive and Thomas Lowe took the parts of Celia and Amiens. It was for Lowe that Arne wrote *Under the Greenwood Tree* and *Blow, blow thou winter wind* and both of these have passed into the common currency of our national song. Curiously enough, the songs *When Daisies pied* and *When Icicles hang by the wall* (*Love's Labour Lost*) were not used in any production of that play, but were introduced into *As you like it*, being sung by Kitty Clive in the character of Celia. It was for Kitty Clive, too, that Arne wrote *Tell me where is fancy bred* (*Merchant of Venice*, 1741) and, again, it was Mrs Clive who took the part of Ariel, *Where the bee sucks*, in *The Tempest* of 1746.

There are two settings of *Come away death* to be noted. The first was sung by Lowe in *Twelfth Night* (1741)[4] but the second is a later and more extended form.[5] One must comment briefly

[1] Op. cit., p. 89.
[2] Both arranged by Guy Warrack (Curwen).
[3] Arranged Adam Carse (Augener).
[4]

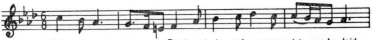

Come a-way, come a-way Death and in sad cy-press let me be laid

Nine Shakespeare Songs, ed. Dr Percy Young (Chappell).

[5]

Come, come, come a-way Death, and in sad cy-press let me be laid

See John Coates Edition (Novello) and *Songs to the Plays of Shakespeare*, ed. Philip Miller (Oxford University Press).

on the remaining, and not so well known, Shakespeare songs by Arne. His *Orpheus with his lute* is, perhaps, a little lame, but the expressive *Dirge* in *Cymbeline*, sung by Lowe as Cadwell at Covent Garden (1759), is far more characteristic. *Pardon Goddess of the Night* (*Much Ado*) is rather angular and *On a day alack the day* (*Love's Labour Lost*) is somewhat indebted to the Scottish 'snap' rhythm, but I feel his *Sigh no more, Ladies* (*Much Ado*) deserves to be better known than it is.

Mackerress has said: 'The London Pleasure Gardens [at Lambeth, Sadler's Wells, Marylebone, Vauxhall and Ranelagh] are of considerable importance to the social history of English music' and they have been accurately described by Frank Kidson as the 'Nurseries of English Song'.[1] It says much for the inclinations of the times that the proprietors of these open-air attractions saw 'an advantage in engaging the services of reputable singers and instrumentalists' while the larger ones also 'favoured the construction of an orchestra around which vocal and instrumentalists could be assembled'. Later on it became a common practice to instal an organ and many organ concertos, especially those of James Hook, were written for performance at Vauxhall.[1] The provinces could also boast similar provision for *al fresco* entertainment.[2] In the meantime, the public concert rooms had increased in number and were mainly devoted to recitals by established artists and visiting foreign musicians seeking wider contacts than friends in private houses, but the limited accommodation of the public concert rooms forced up the prices, whereas in the pleasure gardens people could hear music by Purcell, Handel, Boyce, Arne, Festing and others, under conditions especially provided to attract people of moderate means.

For some ten years from 1745, Arne was director of the music at Ranelagh and it is generally conceded that during his 'reign' the standards of the performances were at their best. And, quite apart from the hundreds of songs he wrote for them,

[1] Op. cit. See also *Invitation to Ranelagh*, Mollie Sands, and *The London Pleasure Gardens of the 18th Century*, Warwick Wroth.

[2] E.g., Newcastle, Birmingham, Bath, Tunbridge Wells and Scarborough.

MICHAEL KELLY, 1762–1826   MRS CROUCH, 1763–1805

JOHN BEARD, *c.* 1717–1791   CHARLES INCLEDON, 1763–1826

THE PLEASURE GARDENS, VAUXHALL, by THOMAS ROWLANDSON

including those for Marylebone and Vauxhall (some forty volumes of these songs were published), he also stands revealed as an outstanding singing teacher, often writing songs expressly for the particular attributes of his pupils, which partly explains the diversity in style of his songs.

This was indeed an age of plenty for English singers, as a perusal of Mollie Sands's *Invitation to Ranelagh* demonstrates, for she offers the most interesting and informative details of an era which stretches virtually from John Beard (the 'first Handelian tenor') to another great tenor of a far different calibre, the tempestuous, unpredictable Charles Incledon, and taking in on the way, as it were, the romantic pairing of Michael Kelly and Mrs Crouch, the extraordinary Mrs Bland, James Bartleman (carrying something of the mantle of Leveridge in Purcell's bass songs) as well as so many others, including the Mrs Martyr for whom Shield wrote his *bravura* song, *Old Towler* (she was also a favourite singer of Hook's songs at Vauxhall) in order to exploit her vocal mannerism, that of a 'staccato style of singing in imitation of Ann Catley, a singer of the previous generation, who caused a sensation by her use of staccato and her charmingly impudent personality'.[1]

One of Arne's earliest pupils was his sister, Susanna Maria, who afterwards became Mrs Cibber and a famous tragic actress. She took the heroine's part in Arne's setting of Addison's *Rosamund* in 1733, while their younger brother, Michael (not to be confused with Arne's son of the same name) took the part of the page. It was this younger brother who wrote *The Lass with the delicate air*, often attributed to Dr Arne. Here, perhaps one may be allowed to take a little of the sting out of a thinly-veiled sneer in *Grove* and repeated by Arthur Jacob in an otherwise outstanding essay on English song.[2] Arne was certainly entitled to be addressed as Doctor Arne, the University of Oxford conferring this title on him in July 1759, and there is no evidence that the composer himself insisted on it. If it was popularly used, it was probably a mark of esteem, even of affection, but never affectation. Arne has suffered more than most from this sort of petty condemnation by critics in

[1] Op. cit.   [2] Op. cit

C

succeeding generations, who fail to recognise his powerful contribution to and influence on English song.

Some of Arne's vituperative letters, like the celebrated one seeking to do new music for a revival of Dryden's *King Arthur* in 1770, deserve opprobrium and suggest personal conceit, but it should be noted also that he waited until the death of Handel before attempting his second oratorio. His first, the *Death of Abel*, was performed in Dublin in 1744, then as *Abel* in Drury Lane in 1755 and at the Haymarket in 1764 under the title of *The Sacrifice*, and is, perhaps, only an average work. But the second, *Judith* (Drury Lane, 1764) is infinitely more confident, despite the poor libretto by Bickerstaffe. The cantabile aria *Sleep Gentle Cherub* is most effective, and two very fine choruses *Who can Schorak's wrath abide* and the finale *Here Sons of Jacob* still hold a place in the choral repertoire. A year later Arne made the bold experiment of 'placing before an English audience an opera composed after the Italian manner, with recitative instead of spoken dialogue'. For this purpose, he selected the *Arteserse* of Metastasio, which he himself translated into English.[1] But he was no poet and we may agree with Herbage that his anglicised Metastasio takes on 'a faint character of burlesque'. But it certainly shows the most confident and varied orchestral scoring he had produced so far and he did find an English equivalent for the Italian florid vocal style. The part of Mandane was specially written for one of his favourite pupils, Charlotte Brent, and it is significant that the opera kept the stage for a good many years. Even now, when it has more or less passed into oblivion, three songs retain their fame, *The soldier tir'd of War's alarms* (still a soprano *tour de force*); *Water parted from the sea* and *In fancy our hopes and fears*. The musical farce *Thomas and Sally* (1760) is undoubtedly a miniature anglicised *opera buffa* with music throughout, and it continues to be a most popular item in the repertoire of the English Intimate Opera Society. Is Herbage right in seeing in these later works of Arne a gravitation towards the style of Mozartian comic opera and, perhaps, something of the mood of Gilbert and Sullivan? It would seem so when we look at Arne's

---

[1] *Grove's Dictionary*, Vol. 1, pp. 209 and 210.

swan song, the comic opera *May Day* (Drury Lane 1775) which was composed with the object of bringing out another of the composer's pupils, Harriet Abrams, one of three famous singing sisters. The libretto, by Garrick, suffers from some weak lyrics, but Arne's long theatrical experience gives a wit and sprightliness to the whole thing and Harriet Abrams's three songs 'are perfect examples of anglicised Italianate melody'.[1]

Perhaps a few more single titles might be noted here of songs which have maintained their place in the singer's repertoire but, as with Purcell, the songs of Arne need a more selective publication in orderly volumes for the singing student, who needs to study them in order to fully appreciate the stylistic qualities of eighteenth-century vocal music. *Despairing beside a clear stream* (a graceful flexible vocal line); *Polly Willis* (quite a favourite in its time); *The Maiden's complaint* (a recitative and sostenuto aria); *When forced from dear Hebe to go* (quite a characteristic song); *Preach not me your musty rules* (a spirited song from *Comus*) and the animated *By the gaily circling glass*. Perhaps mention might also be made here of some important books which were published at this time on musical subjects, like Galliard's English translation of Tosi's *Opinion de cantari antichi e moderni* which greatly influenced all English singing teachers; *Essay on Musical Expression* (Charles Avison), and *The Art of playing on the Violin* (Geminiani) not only because it is reputed to be the first treatise ever printed on the subject, but also because the author was also a highly reputable singing teacher, numbering among his pupils Cecilia Young, who married Arne. Among Arne's 'successors' who must be mentioned were Dr Samuel Arnold, James Hook, Charles Dibdin, Henry Carey, William Shield and J. Stafford Smith. Perhaps the last named has only one claim to fame. His song *To Anacreon in Heaven* was adapted for the *Star Spangled Banner*. Arnold took a lease of Marylebone Gardens and then engaged James Hook as composer and organist. Hook, remembered chiefly for *Sweet Lass of Richmond Hill*, was a most successful composer of light catchy melodies, including *Within a mile of Edinboro' Town*, often quoted in volumes of Scottish national song, as well as

[1] Op. cit.

Lucy Gray of Allendale. It is said that he wrote some 2,000 songs
for Vauxhall Gardens, including things like *Bright Phoebus*;
Love's call; *Softly waft, ye southern breezes* and *The sweet little girl
that I love.*[1] Charles Dibdin was in many ways a remarkable
character who won fame as a singer, author and composer. His
opera, *Liberty Hall*, included such popular songs as *Jack Rattin*;
The High mettled Racer and *The Bells of Aberdovey* while from his
celebrated entertainment *The Oddities*, which ran for a long
season at the Lyceum, came such songs as *Twas on the good ship
Rover*; *Ben Backstay*; *The Lamplighter*; *I sailed from the Downs in
the Navey* and *Tom Bowling*. It was W. Partington who said that
Charles Dibdin was 'the man whose songs helped to win the
battle of Trafalgar and did not allow the nation to forget it
either'.

Henry Carey was thus described by Hawkins, perhaps a little
harshly: 'As a musician, Carey seems to have been one of the
first of the lowest rank, and as a poet, the last of that class of
which D'Urfey was the first.' His claim to the melodies of *Sally
in our Alley* and *God Save the King* both failed, and today he is
only remembered for *Here's to thee my boy* (a rather rowdy
drinking song); *Black-eyed Susan* (which did not gain the
popularity of Leveridge's tune); *Flocks are sporting*, sometimes
called a *Pastoral*, and *The Plausible Lover* (a graceful, delicate
song suitable for light high voices).

William Shield, early made an orphan, pursued his musical
studies with such determination, while serving as apprentice to a
boatbuilder, as to make quite striking progress from the leader-
ship at Scarborough concerts and theatre, to the post of
principal viola at the opera and ultimately his appointment as
Master of the King's Music in 1817. He was responsible, in
whole or in part, for a long list of stage works, in many of which
he introduced songs by various composers, English and foreign.
His own songs are generally quite charming and refined, and
among his most popular are *The Thorn*; *The Wolf*; *The heaving
of the Lead*; *The Post Captain* and *The Ploughboy* (which, curiously
enough, Britten has treated as a folk song). Shield's string music

---

[1] See also *Hail lovely rose*; *The silver moon*; *The cautious maid* &
Trees begin to bud, ed. Ella Ivimey (Augener).

is highly interesting and was much influenced by Haydn, who he said had taught him more in four days than he had learned in any four years of study before. A soprano song *Winds softly tell my love* with accompaniment for *pizzicato* violins seems to merit a modern reprint. Moreover, his *Introduction to Harmony* (1800) and *Rudiments of Thorough-bass* (1815) show that he was a gifted teacher. Stephen Storace was a short-lived genius of outstanding ability. He profited much from an association with Mozart in Vienna, where his sister Nancy had created the part of Susanna in *Figaro*. Soon after his return to London, being offended by the petty jealousies and intrigues of London musical life, he retired to Bath and gave his attention to drawing, for which he had a distinct talent. He resumed his musical pursuits in 1788 and produced several stage works, including an opera *The Haunted Tower* (1789) which had a run of fifty nights in its first season and kept its place in the repertoire for nearly half a century. His charming little opera *No Song no Supper* appeared in 1791.[1] At the time of his death he was engaged on another opera *Mahmoud*, planned for Braham's debut in London. Between them, Michael Kelly and Ann Storace completed the score and it was performed for the benefit of Storace's widow with considerable success. Among the songs of Storace which are still remembered are *Peaceful Slumbering*; *A Sailor loved a lass*; *The Pretty Creature* and *The summer heat's bestowing*. And from his canzonets for voice and piano or harp, *The Curfew* (a setting of words from Gray's *Elegy*) is a striking example, deserving a modern reprint. The Linleys were an important family of musicians, characteristic of many clans of the time, e.g., the Youngs, the Arnes, the Ashleys, etc. Thomas Linley senior was responsible for a great number of stage works, as well as the well-known song *Here's to the Maiden of Bashful Fifteen*.[2] Elizabeth Ann, the elder daughter, was a well-known soprano who married Sheridan. Thomas, the son, was a close friend of Mozart and died at an early age in a boating accident. He contributed songs to a production of *The Tempest* (1789) including *O bid your faithful Ariel fly*.

[1] Now published in the *Musica Britannica Series*.
[2] See also *Still the lark finds repose*, ed. Ivimey (Augener).

We cannot conclude this chapter without a mention of Haydn's *canzonets*, mainly because of his innovation of writing-out the right-hand part of the accompaniment. This change from the usual two-stave song writing in which the accompanist was expected to devise the accompaniment from a bass figured or unfigured with, perhaps, a note or two inserted in the upper stave as a guide, was obviously a thoroughly necessary requirement for the development of the 'art-song' as we understand it today. Though Haydn's *canzonets* cannot be described as master-songs, they won great popularity at the time; e.g., *My Mother bids me bind my hair*; but his *Spirit's Song*; *She never told her love* and the *Sailor's Song* are more typical of him. Finally, Samuel Arnold is chiefly remembered by singers for his *Amo, amas, I love a lass* (a half-Latin song which is really a traditional tune) and his *A clerk I was in London gay* and *Flow thou regal stream*.

5
Victoriana

IT is never very difficult to denigrate the nineteenth century as a whole and the Victorian age in particular in many aspects of human activity. Certainly the musical scene was distressing. But a due debit and credit account might not be so depressing and would, at least, lead to a fairer judgement. In the matter of song, the inheritance was a mixed affair. The fact that our songs had been, since Purcell's day, 'embedded in dramatic pieces', or compiled for anthologies of teaching songs, did not enable the art of song-writing to develop a real artistic identity and in the hands of lesser composers it tended to be somewhat over-simplified as a pleasant melody above a simple accompaniment, or took on a somewhat exaggerated mood of declamatory writing, often to suit the prowess of particular singers. This habit more or less persisted in the first thirty years of the nineteenth century and the fact that the songs of the time are represented by such as *She wore a wreath of roses* by Knight and *I'd be a butterfly* by Haynes Bayly is indicative. These were only two of the many clergymen who entered the lists of song writers about that time. The musical stage productions of the year 1800 are dismal. Covent Garden had been given over 'to the production of sentimental comedies and silly farces, larded with songs and embellished with very flimsy musical pieces'.[1] Little distinction was drawn between ballad-opera and *pasticcio*, and even if these stage shows were seen as a continuation of the masque in an attentuated form (an exceedingly doubtful proposition), a glance at the titles is 'significant of their complete insignificance'.[1] The butchery of Gluck's *Orfeo* (1792) and later

[1] *Music in England*, Eric Blom (Pelican), pp. 126 and 127.

of *Figaro* and *Don Giovanni* reveals to what depths the public taste had sunk.

Eric Blom's succinct observations are worth quoting. 'The last eleven years of George III's active reign, the nine of the Regency, the ten under George IV and the seven under William IV, saw the birth of no English composer of more than moderate distinction, while abroad the years 1803–13 alone produced Berlioz, Mendelssohn, Chopin, Schumann, Liszt, Verdi and Wagner. What is more, the first third of the nineteenth century, or more exactly the first thirty-six and a half years up to the accession of Queen Victoria produced scarcely a British musical work one may designate as bearing the marks of genius, though its composers did contrive to turn out some things that achieved immortality of a kind—the immortality conferred by senti-mental affection, rather than artistic discernment. Bishop's song *Home sweet home* may at once be singled out as a typical product of the kind.'[1]

On the other hand, there is ample evidence of England's immediate acceptance of Beethoven's greatness—not entirely adulatory because it was an English reviewer of the *Septet* who could 'regret the malady of the great composer which deprives the musical world of the pleasure they might have derived from the fruits of his great original genius'. There is, too, an inter-esting comparison of Mozart and Beethoven in the *Quarterly Musical Magazine and Review* (1820) which comments on 'the comparative tameness with which Mozart's most masterly sinfonia in C (No. 1) was received and the applause lavished on Beethoven's in C minor on the fifth night'. The same magazine also contains a letter from one Musicus which says that 'the effect which the writings of Beethoven have had on the art must, I fear, be considered as injurious'. Then there is the outstanding improvement in English orchestral playing. Here we might remark that the Promenade Concert was in existence in various forms from 1830 onwards. One of the earliest 'Prom' conductors was Edward Eliason, a violinist in the Royal Philharmonic orchestra and, indeed, their first soloist in the Beethoven violin concerto. His concerts were given at the Crown and Anchor

[1] Op. cit.

Tavern at the corner of Arundel Street, in the Strand, in a hall which was said to hold over 2,000 people and which had been used for musical events ever since Dr Johnson's time. Nearly always these concerts had a miscellaneous 'second-half' which included solo songs and this was a characteristic of Promenade Concerts down to the 1920s, often providing an opportunity to introduce new songs to an interested public. Nor should we forget the great progress in pianoforte manufacture with which the names of John and James Broadwood and Sebastian Erard are connected, giving a great impetus to the vogue of the newer instrument; and at least two of our singers, Mrs Billington and John Braham were able to win and maintain a Continental reputation. The growth in concert-going was also considerable. These are some of the factors on the credit side.

'The practice of giving oratorio performances at the opera-house during Lent, a practice begun by Handel with such important results, went steadily on, though the word "oratorio" was very liberally interpreted, and secular numbers were often intermixed with sacred.'[1] The Salomon Concerts and the Professional Concerts need no more than a mention here. Their history is well known: the Philharmonic Society which began in 1813 with their concerts in the Argyll Rooms, including chamber music but excluding concertos for any solo instrument, until after the third season; the City Concerts under Sir George Smart were held in the City of London Tavern from 1818 to 1832; the Ancient Concerts (inaugurated 1776), which began in Tottenham Court Road and subsequently moved to the Hanover Square Rooms, flourished until 1848; the Sacred Harmonic Society was an organisation formed for the special purpose of performing oratorios which was started in 1785 and lasted until 1861.

As Fuller-Maitland says, the 'taste of the British public was so much more pronounced in favour of vocal than of instrumental music that the players' names seem much less famous to us in the present day than those of the singers'.[2] To introduce a short consideration of these singers may seem a digression here, since

[1] *English Music in the XIXth Century*, Fuller-Maitland, p. 12.
[2] Op. cit.
C*

their efforts were more devoted to opera and oratorio than to any direct progress in English song itself but they did contribute a great deal to the development of singing technique and are indicative of the musical life of the times. At the beginning of the century, the favourite soprano singers were, apart from Mrs Billington already named, Mme Mara and Mme Catalini as well as a triad of purely English singers, Mrs Salmon, Miss Catherine Stephens and Mary Ann Paton. Mara was a brilliant singer with a large compass and lovely quality. She had a chequered Continental career and her dispute with the Portuguese singer Luiza Todi in Paris was a *cause celebre.* Catalini, who did not always sing in tune, was noted for her profuse cadenzas which showed remarkable agility. Mrs Salmon, a product of Liverpool, had a singularly pure voice but lost her position through intemperate habits. Catherine Stephens, who sang as Mandane in *Artaxerxes* had an unassailable position until her retirement in 1835, when she married the Earl of Essex. Mary Paton, a native of Edinburgh, was something of an infant prodigy. She made her London debut as Susanna in *Figaro* and was the original Agatha in the English version of *Der Freischutz* in 1824. In her early years she tended to imitate Catalini's mannerisms, particularly that of moving her mouth for every note she sang. The contralto voice was little cultivated as such until the advent of Grassini (1773–1850)—she was engaged to sing in London in 1804—because the male alto was used in the concert hall as well as in the cathedral. The favourites were the Knyvetts, father and son,[1] and it is said that they, together with Vaughan and Bartleman, had so perfected their glee singing that 'whoever heard them together, heard the perfection of concerted singing in the species'.[2]

Samuel Harrison was the great tenor of the time, representative of the old style of John Beard. He was at his best in the gentler arias of Handel and was reluctant to attempt the more vigorous. Another tenor, Incledon, has already been mentioned. He was a 'rough diamond', uncommonly good in sea songs (he had been a sailor) but very self-opinionated. The

[1] Cf. in our own day Alfred Deller and his son Mark.
[2] *English Music in the XIXth Century,* J. A. Fuller-Maitland (Grant Richards).

Quarterly Musical Review wrote of him: 'He stopped where he was most pleased and prolonged the passage and the sensation according to the scale of his own satisfaction.' A tenor of the most astonishing popularity was John Braham. As a boy he was noted for his singing of *The soldier tir'd of war's alarms* and sopranos will realise what that means. He had been schooled in the old *bel canto* style but, although he was a poor actor, he brought so much dramatic imagination to his singing that the audience was quite carried away; and it was said that his singing of *Total Eclipse* was a most moving experience. He often wrote his own music for the parts he took in some operas (understandably enough in some cases) and his song *The Death of Nelson*[1] from *The American* had a wide popularity. It was said he introduced a streak of vulgarity into his ballad singing by continuing to introduce long cadenzas and florid passages when such things had fallen out of fashion. He was Max in the English *Der Freischutz* (1824) and the original Sir Huon in *Oberon* (1826). He had a natural son by Nancy Storace in 1801 who took holy orders and became a minor canon, having changed his name to Meadows. Another tenor who must be named is Thomas Vaughan, whose Handelian performances held so much dignity and sincerity as to link his repute with that of Harrison. He sang the tenor solo in the Philharmonic Society's performance of Beethoven's 'Ninth' in 1826.

Of the basses of the time the premier place must be accorded to James Bartleman. He was especially fine in Purcell's songs. There is a legend that he refused to take part in a *Messiah* at which Mozart's added accompaniments were to be used. Such was his repute that these were 'sacrificed' on his account. Richard Bellamy was not only a well-known concert bass but also a theatrical manager of some repute. John Bernard Sale, another well-known bass, was also organist of the Chapel Royal from 1838 and was music tutor to the young Queen Victoria. Lastly there is Henry Phillips, eminently successful both in oratorio and ballad-singing; but not so successful on the stage, although he was Caspar in the English *Der Freischutz* of

---

[1] Which has a remarkable musical identity with Mehul's *Chant du depart.*

1824. In 1843 he started 'table entertainments' in which he was the sole performer. 'He gave these in America and elsewhere with some success, and they undoubtedly set the pattern that was afterwards followed by John Parry, Corney Grain, and others.'[1]

Among the instrumentalists must be named the Ashleys, who seemed to have made orchestral playing a family concern, and J. B. Dando who instigated a series of concerts devoted entirely to string quartets, held at the Hanover Square Rooms from 1835. The best-known cellists were Robert Lindley, famed for his long association with Dragonetti; and Charles Lucas who became Principal of The Royal Academy of Music from 1859 to 1866. And one must name Andrew Ashe, an eminent flute player who became director of the concerts at Bath from 1810 to 1822. Of pianists, the names of Clementi, Pleyel and Moscheles must take precedence, though our home products of John Field and Charles Neate also rank high, and the 'first lady pianist' engaged at the Philharmonic was Mrs Lucy Anderson who was for some time piano tutor to Queen Victoria and her children.

The harp was not then considered an orchestral instrument but as a worthy and popular pursuit for young ladies with shapely arms. A Frenchman, Bochsa, who had fled his country because of his extensive forgeries, was the premier tutor. In England he was better situated. He became professor of the harp and general secretary of the Royal Academy of Music at its institution in 1822. His further claim to notoriety was that in 1839 he ran away with Sir Henry Bishop's wife, with whom he undertook what was virtually a world tour, ending up in Australia where he died in 1856.

Eric Blom's pungent paragraph at the beginning of Chapter IX of his book, *Music in England*, must be quoted here: 'The age of Queen Victoria is as a rule held up to scorn by the modern world, when it does not happen to be the fad of the moment in Chelsea or Bloomsbury. It is regarded as all that is prim, priggish, tasteless and middle-class. True the rise of industrialism and the power of mere wealth resulting from it

[1] Op. cit., p. 23.

gave the more fortunate, the cleverest and also the least scrupulous members of the middle classes their chance to dictate to many people, artists included; and money alone being incapable of raising either taste or sentiment above mediocrity, this new influence encouraged a great deal of valueless production of all kinds. The arts took their share, and more than their legitimate share, in commercial enterprise.' We have seen that the lowering of standards in musical stage shows had started towards the end of the previous century, so that the tasteless progress of Bishop and his ilk was only continuing a trend which had already begun. Even the fine traditions of English Church music showed some signs of weakness, partly because the term 'sacred music' took on an odd connotation. As for English song, the success and popularity of the pleasure gardens was something of a two-edged sword, with music becoming more of an entertainment than an art, and singers eager to court popularity even by doubtful means. Had England been possessed of composers of the calibre of, say, Beethoven, Schubert, Schumann and Brahms (she already possessed the poets) English song might have challenged German *Lieder*. But we were destined to traverse the morass of Victorian song before the faintest signs of artistic progress were to be discerned. The significant extension of interest in the amateur sector—the educational impulse of the Mainzer, Hullah and Curwen methods and the early signs of the brass band movement, for example—held a tinge of 'social welfare' as a stronger motive, perhaps, than artistic progress; but we must not forget the potent influence of family music-making where the 'parlour' took on something of the character of the aristocratic salon in more humble style.

The cult of the English Glee offers a strongly contrasted effort. Here was a choral activity essentially English and predominantly male, which had no use for doggerel. Recalling something akin to the madrigal era, it had a like length of active existence—a little less than a century from 1750 to 1850. Towards the end they were getting nearer to the part-song style, but in its hey-day the glee was strikingly individual. Examples like Webbe's *Glorious Apollo*, Danby's *Awake Aeolian Lyre*, Stevens's *From Oberon* and William Paxton's *Breathe soft*,

Ave Maria

Attwood

ye winds are masterpieces of their kind. And in the matter of performance, as any member of an existing glee club will testify, standards are good, and it is not to be wondered at as the performers are so often lay clerks or vicars-choral of a cathedral. Only in the American counterparts of these glee clubs are banjos and mandolins allowed to invade this province of unaccompanied part-singing.

In passing, we must mention two songs by Charles Edward Horn, a singer[1] and composer of German descent: *I've been roaming* and *Cherry Ripe* which were very popular in their day, as was Hullah's *Three fishers went sailing*, but a more interesting and important song was a setting of Scott's poem *Ellen's Song* or *Ave Maria* by Attwood, anticipating Schubert by some fifteen years, not only because of its thoroughly pianistic accompaniment and its bold harmonies, but also its due sense of poetic atmosphere, as can be seen from the quotation given here (p. 78). One feels strongly that this song deserves a modern reprint. And this brings us to another remarkable comparison with Schubert, that of Loder's setting of a translation by Longfellow of *Wohin*, under the title *The Brooklet*.[2] It is characteristic of the times that the composer, who had studied in Germany under Ferdinand Ries, and at one time contemplated taking up medicine, was, on his return to England, commissioned to write a new song each week by the publishers, Dalmaine & Co., which produced a most unequal output, including such items as *The Diver*, and *The old house at home*. 'As it became necessary that some of the pieces produced under this arrangement, should be heard in public, an opera entitled *Francis I* was written to incorporate them and produced at Drury Lane in 1838. So heterogeneous a compound met with little success.'[3] Loder's best stage work, *The Night Dancers*, was produced at the Princess's Theatre in 1845 and revived at

---

[1] His voice was so extensive in compass, that he could undertake both tenor and baritone parts.

[2] Now published in *New Imperial Album for Tenor* (Boosey & Hawkes), p. 50, and separately under the title *I heard a brooklet gushing* (Oxford Press).

[3] *Grove's Dictionary*, Vol. V, p. 357.

SIR CHARLES VILLIERS STANFORD, 1852–1924

SIR C. HUBERT PARRY, 1841–1924

JENNY LIND (1820–1887) AT EXETER HALL IN 1853
from 'The Mirror of Music' edited by Percy Scholes

Covent Garden in 1860, having already had performances in New York and Australia.

With a taste for the Victorian conventional ballad, as Arthur Jacob has pointed out, 'went a taste for things a good deal better'. Songs by Schubert, Haydn and Schumann appeared in Victorian song albums, side by side with Knight's *She wore a wreath of Roses*. Indeed, it would be a mistake to deride completely the popular taste. True, it produced a bevy of lyric writers like John Oxenford, W. H. Weiss, F. E. Weatherley, Mrs G. Hubi-Newcombe. If the last-named was the most prolific, it must be remarked that Weatherly had been an Oxford tutor, was a K.C. and the author of *The Rudiments of Logic Induction and Deduction*, while Oxenford had some repute as a translator. And, before denouncing these authors entirely, we might remember that Mollie Sands could say of the words to some eighteenth-century song at the pleasure gardens: 'The Damons, the Strephons, and the Colins, the Hebes, the Sylvias and the Chloes, tell the stories of their pastoral loves in verses which invariably rhyme "swain" with "plain" and "love" with "rove".' It is not difficult to name the 'top ten' among the Victorian song composers. Undoubtedly the most prolific and the most successful was Stephen Adams (né Michael Maybrick), so successful as to drop from the music dictionaries. Many of his songs had phenomenal sales, like *Mona*, *Nirvana*, *Thora*, *The Midshipmite* and *The Holy City*, reaching 50,000 copies per annum. And it was the eminent Victorian tenor, Edward Lloyd, who left on record the fact that in Montreal he was engaged four times in one month at a fee of 250 guineas each concert, on condition that he sang *The Holy City* on each occasion. Other household names were Ciro Pinsuti, Piccolomini (really a Dublin-born Frenchman), Blumenthal, Molloy, Mascharoni (the copyright of whose song *For all Eternity*, popularised by Patti, was sold by auction for £2,240), Cowen, Lohr, Trotere (né Trotter) and Francis Allitsen (whose patriotic song *There's a Land* was immensely popular during the South African War).

The revulsion against these songs is now so complete, perhaps, that it would be idle to name even the more musically meritorious; but it can be said that the vocal melodies, if full of

certain clichés, were grateful to the voice and the sickly sentiments were often more verbal than musical. Singers of high
technical accomplishment could often bring an artistic dignity
to their performance, and anyone who heard the late John
McCormack singing *Il mio tesoro* and *Macushla* in the same
programme would have to acknowledge the artistic skill he
was able to bring to each.

For all the popularity of the Victorian ballad, it was but a
small feature of a fairly vigorous and varied pursuit of music.
To consider the whole musical scene, often illumined and
influenced by the visitations and sojourns of many eminent
foreign musicians, is hardly possible within the confines of a
single chapter. The reader can be referred to Dr Scholes's
Mirror of Music (two Vols., Novello) which offers a comprehensive and detailed survey of a 'century (1844-1944) of musical
life in Britain as reflected in the pages of the *Musical Times*'.
Clearly we are mainly concerned here with those features which
concern song and/or singers. For example, opera. Fashionable
audiences continued to support Italian opera in the Haymarket. But at Drury Lane Alfred Bunn tried commissioning
and producing native works in English from about 1838
onwards, e.g., Balfe's *Bohemian Girl*, Benedict's *Brides of Venice*
and Wallace's *Maritana*. In 1847 Italian opera transferred from
the Haymarket to Covent Garden. The long and disastrous
rivalries between the theatres need not concern us here, except
to observe that manager after manager was ruined in the
process. Even Monck Mason who tried a series of German
opera, including the first performance of *Fidelio* in England with
Schroeder Devrient in the title role, found the fashionable
audiences were fickle and prone to rather snobbish preferences.
However, Meyerbeer's *Les Huguenots* was produced at both
theatres in 1858. There was also a famous performance of
Cimarosa's *Matrimonio Segreto* in 1841, with Grisi, Persiani
Viardot, Rubini, Tamburini and Lablache, which, says Fuller-
Maitland, must have been the highest point of ensemble ever
attained in operatic annals. We must note, too, the debuts of
Patti and Faure in 1860, of Santley in 1862, and of Lucca in
1863 at Covent Garden. And since *Faust* had been turned down
by the Garden on more than one occasion, they must have

looked with mixed feelings on its success at Her Majesty's. After the burning of Her Majesty's, there was a 'coalition' season in 1869 which brought about a 'famous performance of *Don Giovanni* although Costa was absent from the post of conductor, which he had filled so well'. When Her Majesty's was rebuilt, it was at first used for the religious meetings of Moody and Sankey.

We must not forget the enterprise of the singers Pyne and Harrison at the Lyceum, Drury Lane and Covent Garden. It resulted in the production of Benedict's *Lily of Killarney* and some excellent English productions of French opera. Their association lasted from 1856 to 1864. A much more significant enterprise was the foundation of the Carl Rosa Opera Company in 1875. It opened at the Princess's Theatre in Oxford Street, and constantly toured the whole country in between regular London seasons. Among some of their more important productions were *Flying Dutchman* with Charles Santley in 1876, *Rienzi* (at Her Majesty's 1879) as well as introducing English audiences to Goetz's *Taming of the Shrew*. The company, who were accorded the prefix 'Royal' by Queen Victoria in 1893, not only included in its large repertory the well-known works by Balfe, Wallace and Benedict, but also commissioned new works by Mackenzie, Stanford, Cowen, Corder and MacCunn, as well as performing in English most of the standard Italian, French and German operas. It is regrettable that this fine company should have been brought to an untimely end in our own day by a lack of imagination by some of our bureaucrats. Finally, another enterprise by two singers, Fanny Moody and Charles Manners, must be noted. The Moody Manners Opera Company was founded in 1897 and at one time had three companies on the road, one visiting U.S.A., Canada and South Africa. They enjoyed successful London seasons at Covent Garden in 1902 and 1903, and at Drury Lane in 1904. It ended its career in 1913. The company, like the Royal Carl Rosa, was an important training ground for British opera singers, and its passing, together with that of the Rosa, leaves a conspicuous gap.

It was in 1875 that a London concert agent, Rupert D'Oyly Carte, who had an interest in French opera (by Lecocq, Offenbach and others) fell in with a suggestion that he should get Arthur Sullivan to write a curtain-raiser. Already Sullivan had a certain repute as a writer of some orchestral music, an oratorio (*The Prodigal Son*) and a little opera *Cox and Box* to a libretto by F. C. Burnand, the editor of *Punch*. The work chosen as the curtain-raiser was *Trial by Jury* to a libretto by W. S. Gilbert with whom Sullivan had previously combined in *Thespis*, or *The Gods grown old* at the Gaiety Theatre in 1871. But now began a famous partnership which is too well-known to recount here. It led to the formation of a syndicate and the building of a theatre and so the *genus* Savoy Operas was well and truly established. *The Sorcerer* (1877), *H.M.S. Pinafore* (1878), *The Pirates of Penzance* (1880), *Patience* (1881), *Iolanthe* (1882), *Princess Ida* (1884), *The Mikado* (1885), *Ruddigore* (1887), *Yeomen of the Guard* (1888), *The Gondoliers* (1889), is a list of successes which were phenomenal. 'Apart from their pecuniary value, the work achieved by these operas was undoubtedly to alter the condition of music in England as regarded by the average member of the public. Instead of being a thing apart from his daily life, or a set of taking tunes associated with sentimental or convivial words, here were pieces which the average man could grasp as a whole, and yet which so delighted musicians by their refinement, cleverness, and sparkling effect, that both classes could mingle their enthusiasms.'[1] Undoubtedly, those of Sullivan's admirers who press his claims to be considered as a 'serious' composer (in the narrow sense of that word) hardly do him justice. In his serious works he was too inconsistent and often lacking in taste. Many of his songs, except the Shakespeare songs and *The loves of the wrens* to words expressly written for Sullivan at the request of Sir George Grove, often descend to the sentimental and even the vulgar.[2] But the Savoy Operas are sufficient to carry him to immortality, especially now that they are relieved of the mechanically stylised production which has type-cast them for so long, although it must be admitted that the 'new productions' are slow in gaining acceptance.

[1] *English Music in the XIXth Century*, Fuller Maitland, p. 173.

[2] *Orpheus with his lute* and *The Willow song* are perhaps the best of a set of five which also includes *O Mistress Mine*, *Rosalind* and *Sigh no more ladies*. The Tennyson cycle is particularly beautiful.

It is curious that some of the operas not connected with Gilbert, such as *Haddon Hall* (1892), *The Chieftain* (1894), *The Beauty Stone* (1898) did not have the same measure of success. *The Rose of Persia* (1899) to a libretto by Basil Hood was more favourably accepted and *The Emerald Isle*, which was completed by Edward German after Sullivan's death in 1900, was also quite well received. The hopes that were pinned on a 'grand' opera by Sullivan in The English Opera House were not fully realised. *Ivanhoe*, to a libretto by Julian Sturgis, tended to be a 'jumble of heterogeneous materials', although the opera itself was more successful than the overall venture of the Opera House. Blom has rightly described Sullivan, in the realm of light opera, as 'an inexhaustible melodic inventor, an incomparably graceful and accomplished craftsman and a comic artist of endless wit and versatility'.[1] And he was a master of musical parody, e.g. Mad Meg's song in *Ruddigore*. He was also a master of orchestration. 'He could make a small orchestra sound astonishingly full and satisfying without sacrificing a delightful lucidity and this was largely a technical matter of skilful distribution and spacing.'[1]

In the province of oratorio—and this was veritably a century of oratorio performance—English composers seemed to have more activity to offer, stimulated, of course, by the great choral festivals which were a marked feature of the times. Handel was the dominant figure and remained so for a long time. The successful performance of Haydn's *Creation* at Covent Garden in 1800 had brought a new name into the repertory, but his *Seasons* was not so quickly acclaimed. Mendelssohn with his *Hymn of Praise* (1840), *St Paul* (1836), and *Elijah* (1846)—the dates are those of first performance in England—soon became a serious rival to Handel with a work which Donald Tovey has said 'musically and dramatically, towers above later works by many accomplished composers who despise it'.[2] Of English oratorio there is no significant work between Arne's *Judith* (1761) and Crotch's *Palestine* (1812) but some foreign composers early made an impression, for example, Spohr and

[1] *Grove's Dictionary*, Vol. VIII, pp. 180 and 181.
[2] *Musical articles from Enc. Brit.*, Donald F. Tovey, p. 161.

Rossini. Spohr's *Calvary* (Norwich 1839) incurred the opposition of the clergy because 'of the intimate treatment of its libretto'. His *Last Judgment* was quickly accepted and became his most popular work. Incidentally, the *Musical News* of April 1903 reporting on a performance in a Glamorganshire village church, said it had been announced by a notice on the church door which read: 'On Sunday next the choir will give a performance of Spohr's *Last Judgment*. The church will be specially heated for the occasion.' It is not easy to trace first performances in England of some of these foreign works, but the comparative lists of performances compiled by the *Musical Times* and quoted by Dr Scholes[1] gives some idea of the extent of the 'invasion'.

What is rather surprising is the belated recognition of the three Bs.—Bach, Beethoven and Brahms—in religious choral music. The slow acceptance of Bach, despite the energies of such ardent champions as Barnby, Wesley, Sterndale Bennett and Mendelssohn himself, can be seen from the fact that while Wesley put on a performance of *Jesu Meine Freude* at a Morning Musical Party at Hanover Square Rooms in 1809, no other performance of Bach is to be traced until the inclusion of the duet and chorus, *My Saviour, now is taken* (St Matthew) as an item in the Birmingham Festival programme of 1837. In 1838 the Choral Harmonist's Society included the CREDO from the first *Grand Mass* by which they obviously mean the *B minor*. In 1851 Hullah also performed the CREDO and a year later the MAGNIFICAT had its first English performance, though a private one, when John Stainer, a St Paul's choir boy, sang the alto part. In 1854 the New Philharmonic Society gave a short selection from the *Matthew Passion* at St Martin's Hall and in the same year the Bach Society gave what is generally described as the first performance in England of the *St Matthew Passion*, conducted by Sterndale Bennett. The Bach Society further justified its title by giving the first eleven movements of the *B minor* in 1860 and also the first British performance of the *Christmas Oratorio* in 1861. And in the following year they published by subscription an English edition of the *St Matthew Passion* edited by Sterndale Bennett to a translation by Helen Johnston. This

---

[1] *The Mirror of Music*, ed. Scholes, Vol. 1, pp. 146–7.

enabled Barnby in 1870 to present the whole work to the normal oratorio public at St James's Hall, and it was in 1871 that the work was admitted to the programme of the Gloucester Festival. The *St Matthew Passion* was now 'fairly floated and efforts were obviously called for to push the *Mass in B minor* into the channels of public performance and appreciation'.[1] This the Bach Choir (formed in 1875) was very soon able to do, and thanks to the enterprise of Otto Goldschmidt (the husband of Jenny Lind), a performance took place in St James's Hall in April 1876, the first of many. Beethoven met a curious fate. His *Mount of Olives* was first introduced to this country by Sir George Smart in his Lenten concerts at Drury Lane as early as 1814. Some religious purists objected to the actual personality and voice of Christ being used, and in 1842 a Dr Hudson of Dublin 'swept Christ right out of the score, substituting an entirely new book of Old Testament unobjectionability under the title of *Engedi, or David in the Wilderness*', and it was so given as late as 1905 at the Bristol Festival. It was at the Leeds Festival of 1877 that a translation of the original libretto was introduced. The *Mass in D* had a certain number of performances, but with such mutilations that Barnby, in giving two performances at St James's Hall in 1870, had to state that there was to be no curtailment or alteration, and that the two performances represented the 'first time in this country without alteration or curtailment'.[2] The first performances of Brahms's *Requiem* were those by students of the Royal Academy of Music under Hullah in Hanover Square Rooms, and by the Philharmonic Society under Cusins in St James's Hall on consecutive evenings in April 1873.

The speedy and favoured acceptance of Spohr (and Gounod) and the slow acceptance of Bach are, perhaps, symptomatic of the age. Victorian piety was sentimentally self indulgent, and could respond to the cloying nature of the *Last Judgment* and *Redemption* far more easily than to the sensitive and penetrating character of Bach. The tremendous popularity of 'sacred' songs like *The Better Land* (Cowen), *Abide with me* (Liddle), is only a further proof of this weakness. Even *Elijah* could be

[1] Op. cit.   [2] Op. cit.

sentimentalised, as Stanford discovered and commented on in a letter to *The Times* (7 December 1901): 'I had always heard from certain of Mendelssohn's pupils whom I knew, that he was most careful and precise in his metronome marks, and not long before I visited Mr Lockey,[1] I rehearsed the oratorio with an orchestra which would scarcely believe that my *tempi* were sane until I produced a metronome to verify them. The general tendency had been to sentimentalise the *Andantes* and to reduce the fiery speed of the quick movements. When I saw Mr Lockey I asked him to hum for me the most obvious cases as nearly as he could recall in the composer's *tempi*, and in every instance his pace was that of the metronome. The most striking modern lapses are in the contralto airs "Woe unto them" and especially "O rest in the Lord". The latter air was sung in 1846 by Miss Williams who afterwards married Mr Lockey. He told me that Mendelssohn impressed upon her the importance of singing this song quite simply and without dragging. It is now frequently reduced to nearly half speed. He also mentioned the prodigious pace of the final Baal chorus and of the song "Is not his word like a fire", in two movements of which (as my father told me) Mendelssohn's conducting was like whipping cream. I then told Lockey of the modern fashion, beloved of solo tenors, of making a sweeping *portamento* at the return of the opening theme in "If with all your hearts", and asked him if it was traditional. Lockey threw up his hands with horror at the idea, and told me that Mendelssohn impressed upon him again and again the vital importance of perfect simplicity in singing this air.'

So, it was perhaps inevitable that English oratorio of the nineteenth century, though extensive in quantity should be doubtful in quality and had to wait until the last decade of the century for some signs of improvement. Bennett's *Woman of Samaria*, Macfarren's *St John the Baptist*, and Pierson's *Jerusalem* (with a touch of revolutionary boldness) are perhaps the best examples from a period which has earned somewhat trenchant comments. Dr Ernest Walker has written: 'With Arne's death in 1775, English oratorio music entered on a century of artistic

[1] Mr Lockey was the tenor soloist in the first performance conducted by the composer.

darkness over which brooded from first to last the elephantine shadow of Handel, to which was added in the final thirty years the almost equally ostentatiously ponderous shadow of Mendelssohn. The composers of these tons of oratorios were all "honourable men". . . . They worked hard and conscientiously, and their music is nothing worse than intolerably dull. They set well-nigh every word of the Bible; and when they were not writing oratorios of their own, they were still making them out of the mangled remains of other men's music.'[1] Sir Donald Tovey strikes another note: 'In England the influence of Mendelssohn completed the devastation begun by our inveterate habit of praising the inspired literary skill of the sacred narrative as a preface to our restatement of it in forty times as many words of our own. Deans and chapters listened in graceful official pride and imperfectly secret glee to the strains in which the cathedral organist celebrated with equal realism the destruction of Sennacherib's hosts and his own octuply-contrapuntal doctorate of music.'[2]

In some ways, the history of the oratorio is that of a changing choral art-form with somewhat vague boundaries. Three kinds of development emerge. (a) Purely worship-music which reaches the dimensions of what may be termed the concert-mass; (b) the cult of the Biblical narrative which opens the way for the extended secular cantata and (c) the choral forms associated with settings of poetry of a lofty kind, though not necessarily religious. The last category is easily recognised as that of the modern 'oratorio' from *Gerontius* onwards. The increasing number and importance of these choral festivals from about 1860 onwards was most gratifying.[3] To the university and cathedral occasions was added the sponsorship of some of the commercial and industrial centres, e.g., Birmingham, Wolverhampton, Staffordshire (potteries), Leeds, Bristol, Glasgow, etc.[4] Undoubtedly, choral England was showing its

[1] *Grove's Dictionary*, Vol. VI, pp. 60–1.
[2] *Musical articles from Enc. Brit.*, Donald F. Tovey (Oxford), p. 162.
[3] See *The Mirror of Music*, ed. Scholes, Vol. I, p. 158 f.
[4] See Translation of Otto Lessman's article *Musical Times*, November 1889.

most impressive form and possessed solo singers of the right eminence to sustain them. Perhaps a list of some of the leading singers of the whole era may be of interest. Among the sopranos were Clara Novello, Anne Bishop, Susan Sykes (Mrs Sunderland), Louise Pyne, Edith Wynne, Jessy Bond, Liza Lehmann, Fanny Moody, Nellie Melba, Agnes Nichols and Ruth Vincent. Among mezzos: Mary Davies, Alice Gomez, Marie Brema, Kirkby Lunn and Muriel Foster. Contraltos included Mary Postans, Charlotte Sainton Dolby, Janet Patey, Mary Wakefield, Clara Butt, Phyllis Lett, Ada Crossley, and Edna Thornton. Among the tenors we must name Sims Reeves, Charles Lockey, W. H. Cummings, Edward Lloyd, William Shakespeare, Courtice Pounds, Ben Davies, Gregory Hast and John Coates. From a fairly substantial list of baritones one would cite Henry Phillips, Charles Santley, Andrew Black, Bantock Pierpoint, Frangcon Davies, Charles Knowles, Kennerley Rumford and Charles Tree: and basses include Frank Celli, 'Signor' Foli (né Allen James Foley), Charles Manners, Bertram Mills, Plunket Greene, Harry Dearth and Robert Radford. These were English singers who undoubtedly earned a great repute as much for their vocal resource as for their interpretative sensitivity even if, to satisfy the fashion of the time, they were compelled to admit into the repertory some songs of doubtful worth.

The year 1880 has been conveniently fixed to mark what has been called the Renaissance in British music. The title may be, as Arthur Jacob has said, 'an overstatement', though not for the reasons he gives. In the matter of choral and vocal music it was certainly a turning point with a revaluation in taste and style which was destined to have a considerable influence on the future. And it must be connected with three illustrious names: Parry, Stanford and Elgar. Although Parry's *Prometheus Unbound* (Gloucester, 1880) met with a mixed reception at its first performance, it is still, in many respects, one of his finest works and its qualities of style and character are equally plain in the later *Glories of our Blood and State* (1885 revised 1914), *Blest Pair of Sirens* (1887) and *L'Allegro* (1890). Parry's affinity with Milton is not without significance. So, too, his oratorios *Judith* (1888) and *Job* (1892) which were strides ahead of their predecessors. It was Dr Ernest Walker who wrote: 'There is real nobility of manner about the finest specimens of his broad choral writing, with its powerful, dignified climaxes—nobility of a kind that is the reverse of common in English or any other composition',[1] and this noble spirit marks even his slighter compositions, e.g., *England, Jerusalem*, as well as the deeply moving *Songs of Farewell* (1916–18). It has been said that Bach and Brahms, with perhaps a hint of Handel and Mendelssohn, were the sources of Parry's style, but we must not forget the practical influence of Dannreuther. More surely, Parry was strongly individual and students who came under his beneficent sway at the Royal College of Music will recognise in the bluff humour of his *Pied Piper* (1905) the poetic sensuousness of his *Lotus Eaters* (1892), the philosophic profundity of *War and Peace* (1903), spiritual tranquility of his *Beyond these Voices there is Peace* (1908), many of the characteristics that went to the making of this genial and genuine personality.

Naturally, it is with Parry's songs that we are most concerned in this book. He wrote about 150 in all, the majority of them, in *Twelve sets of English Lyrics*. His early songs, such as *The Poet's Song, Music, Autumn, The River of Life* and *Twilight* are delightfully fresh and melodious. The settings of Four Shakespeare Sonnets are not wholly successful for all the appeal of *Shall I compare thee*. Six Shakespeare songs also comprise Set II of the *English Lyrics*, though none are as engaging as his *On a day alack the day* and *Crabbed age and Youth* (Set V). His sympathetic understanding of Mary Coleridge's poetry makes Set IX the most attractive, containing as it does *A Fairy Town, Armida's Garden* and *The Maiden*. *Follow a shadow* (Set VII) has a delightfully well pointed and genial humour to compare with the rhythmic vigour of *Love is a Bable* (VI) and a haunting sense of atmosphere makes *Dirge in Woods*, to Meredith's words, one of his most striking songs. The vivacious *Birthday* (Rossetti) from Set X, the charming *Lover's Garland* (VI) and the gently serious *Through The Ivory Gate* (III) are also singularly attractive.

There will be those who deem Parry's songs as too unequal to be really outstanding, and admittedly some of his piano

---

[1] *History of Music in England*, E. Walker, p. 331.

accompaniments are rather angular; despite which I often find a curious affinity with Schumann in his vocal writing. But his songs are essentially English and his emotional refinement, together with his pre-occupation with correct declamation, were to be notable influences on the succeeding generations of song-composers.

The character and prowess of Charles Villiers Stanford can never be contained within a few paragraphs of prose. He was, in the words of Dr Herbert Howells, 'a paramount figure that for forty years had been a major driving force in the creative and interpretative life of the nation's music'.[1] His immediate contributions to the Renaissance might be listed as *The veiled prophet of Khorassan* (1881), *The Three Holy Children* (1885), *The Revenge* (1886), *The Voyage of Maeldune* (1889), but these are only the titles of the early stirrings of that creative genius that was to bring us a frighteningly long catalogue of works, far-ranging in extent, and far-reaching in influence. Dr Herbert Howells' centenary address to the Royal Musical Association in December 1952 deserves our closest scrutiny if we would understand and appreciate this remarkable character. He touched our music at all points: choral and instrumental, Church and chamber, to say nothing of his operas and, happily for our present purpose, in full and astonishing fecundity in the realm of song. He wrote over 160 songs, including a dozen settings of Heine's poems published in 1892, though probably written much earlier. To quote Howells again: 'By their subtlety and fine-spun texture, their general reticence, their high sensitivity to the colours, tensions and characteristics of even our most hackneyed words, and by their astonishing flair for the placing and changes of emphasis in any single phrase or succession of phrases—by any of these criteria—the songs are rare and lovely things.'[1]

I had contemplated presenting here a complete list of Stanford's songs, but as such a list can be consulted in *Grove's Dictionary* as well as under various publishers in the Appendix to this book, it is hardly necessary.[2] Instead, perhaps we might take

---

[1] *Proc. Royal Mus. Ass.*, Vol. 79, 1952–3.
[2] *Grove's Dictionary*, Vol. VIII, pp. 54–5.

a glance at some of his better-known items to try and discover some of the details of his creative skill. We might acknowledge, for example, the infinite tenderness of his *Johneen*; the gaunt and graphic declamation of *The Pibroch*; the racy realism of his *Bold Unbiddable Child*; the classical dignity of the memory-laden threnody *Heraclitus*; the dreamy impressionism of the *Fairy Lough*; the simple but so graphic atmosphere of *A Soft Day* and so on. It must be realised that in his songs, Stanford's vocal lines are always evocative rather than dramatic in their poetic realism and they are surely infinite in their melodic variety. If we compare Stanford's setting of *Sea Wrack* with that by Hamilton Harty, which is a masterpiece anyway, we might glean something of Stanford's individual sensitivity and subtlety in evoking the maximum effect with the minimum of musical means. So often a tiny melodic quirk or a singularly apt rhythmic figure suffices to paint a vivid detail, whether it be the 'fairy horsemen' of the *Fairy Lough*, the proud and bluff bearing of the *Little Admiral*, the toiling perseverance of *The Old Superb*, the stark emotion of *The Monkey's Carol* (for me curiously reminiscent of *Der Leiermann* in some ways) or the poignant nostalgia of *Homeward Bound*. His musical imagery is so purposeful and carefully pointed that the singer must beware of exaggerated expression, allowing the song to 'sing itself' almost, to the lilt of the composer's natural and spontaneous lyricism. It is singularly fortunate for English song that, as a teacher, Stanford was able to pass on some of these qualities, particularly his directness of purpose, his rare musical imagery and, above all, his effective economy of means, to our younger composers.

The third and youngest member of the trio was Edward Elgar, who first manifested his power with the overture *Froissart* (Worcester, 1890), and at once revealed himself as a composer who did not so much score for an orchestra, but actually *thought* in its terms. There followed *The Black Knight* (Worcester, 1895) and the *Choral Suite* from the *Bavarian Highlands*. His first oratorio was *The Light of Life* (Worcester, 1896). *King Olaf* belongs to the same year, though it was first produced at Hanley. Elgar's songs are far from being what one hopes. Perhaps Newman was right, when he said they belonged to the composer's off-moments when he was not working on the large choral or orchestral canvas. Even the celebrated *Sea Pictures* were trenchantly criticised by Newman. His non-success in this direction is the more puzzling when one thinks of the excellent song of the Angel in *Gerontius* and the charming songs in *The Starlight Express*, the Christmas play by Algernon Blackwood for which Elgar wrote the incidental music. The morbid solemnity of Wastell's *Like to the damask rose* is not exactly an inspiring affair for a song-writer and it led Elgar to some misguided exaggerations which a certain type of singer revels in. The popular *Shepherd's Song* for all its charm hardly lives up to the airy ecstasy of Barry Pain's pastoral. One of his most satisfying songs is the tenor *Is she not passing fair*, although the same opus number includes *Pleading*, which is not much more than a drawing-room ballad.

We have long since reached the turn of the century and many of the songs which have been cited may seem to belong more properly to the next chapter. But it is never very easy to choose the exact moment of change in the progress of Art. The new century began with a tremendous musical promise, particularly in the matter of song, as we shall see.

6

The Twentieth Century

ANY attempt to establish positive links between English song of the eighteenth, nineteenth and twentieth centuries would be pointless, even if it could be made plausible. True, the traditional song collections of the earlier centuries afford proof 'that the popularity of song was never lost in England'; but there is little evidence that these earlier songs exercised much influence on the later song writers, either in style or character. The circumstances and musical motives of each age were fundamentally different, as we have seen. For example, the pastoral love life of the Hebes and Strephons and the blatant patriotism which characterised so many of the songs which won popular acclaim in the pleasure gardens of Vauxhall and Ranelagh would not have been as well received in the Victorian drawing-room as were their own sentimental ballads, and *vice versa*. But the Victorian tradition of family music, sometimes mockingly described as 'parlour-culture' was a most suitable milieu for the subsequent development of song in the Edwardian epoch, when higher standards started to emerge and English song began to establish a certain artistic and musical identity. Indeed the first half of the twentieth century was such a prolific and progressive period that to organise a survey of so varied a catalogue was by no means easy. I confess to making several attempts. Because I deemed that my avowed purpose was to bring to critical notice as much as possible of this diverse corpus of English vocal music, I soon decided that to attempt a purely chronological scheme would serve no useful purpose; but I felt that by dividing the impulse into three main streams of effort, with allowances for some cross-reference of categories, it would make for reasonable clarity and order. And if I have been guilty of allowing my argument to be swayed more by the warm enthusiasms of a singer than the cool judgement of musical erudition, I am unrepentant. The time has surely come when our singers and singing teachers should be prevailed upon to investigate more closely and constructively their native inheritance of song at its best and most plentiful.

To begin with, one must acknowledge the continued domination of the drawing-room ballad, though of a vastly improved quality as compared with the Victorians. True, there were still a few composers who showed little advance. But we can assume, probably, that Tosti gained his knighthood in 1908 for his talent as vocal teacher to the Royal family, rather than for his taste (or lack of it) in writing songs. A composer like Wilfred Sanderson, who may seem to have donned the mantle of Stephen Adams, was a reasonably competent composer and among his long list of frankly popular ballads are one or two examples of better things, e.g., *Drake goes West*, *The Laughing Cavalier* and *Charm me asleep*. At least three or four women composers must come into our discussion here. Maude Valerie White attained a distinct popularity with *The Devout Lover* and *King Charles*, both of which have a certain merit. And the extremely popular *Indian Love Lyrics* by Amy Woodford Finden should not be utterly disdained because they are distinctly dated. Teresa del Riego (*Homing*, *Remembrance* and *Resurrection*) too, is not without a certain merit. Liza Lehmann, with her song cycle *In a Persian Garden* for vocal ensemble as well as solo voices, and her group of *Bird Songs* and *If I built a world for you* can hardly be denied a respectable niche in a survey of English song. Maurice Besly, who has many drawing-room ballads to his name, has also written two quite distinguished art songs in his *Epitaph* and *Listening*. Similarly, Landon Ronald's songs *Down in the Forest* and *O Lovely Sleep* are in strong contrast with his setting of Shelley's *Adonais*, a scena for voice and orchestra. The felicitous talents of Eric Coates (*Bird songs at Eventide*), Haydn Wood (*Roses of Picardy*) and Montague Philips (*Fisherman of England*), are all examples of undoubted craftsmanship, even if they succumb to the blandishments of popular taste.

Several composers managed to keep a foot in both camps, of

drawing-room ballad and art song, with a certain measure of success. As, for example, Graham Peel, whose list of attractive and popular songs includes a setting of *In Summertime on Bredon* which ranks high in comparison with other settings of this poem of Housman's; while Frederick Keel's admirable settings of Masefield's *Salt Water Ballads* have undeniable quality while retaining a distinctive and direct appeal and attractiveness. And we might reflect that lowly as the motives of the drawing-room ballad might be, it never cultivated an American accent and it has merits which are completely absent from the contemporary commercial popular song. At least its pursuit is recognisable as singing, which is more than can be said for the 'pop' song of today, except on very rare occasions.

Our second stream of progress, therefore, concerns the general development of the English art song in all its simpler forms and if, now and again, an occasional example seems to look over its shoulder towards the drawing-room *genre*, it may be none the worse for that. Song is, after all, so much of an amateur pursuit and an active exercise rather than an academic one. We are, of course, immediately confronted with the problem of finding acceptable definitions of 'drawing-room ballad' and 'art song'. Most people will say they know what they mean by the terms, and that it is all a matter of quality (or is it of opinion?). I once heard a reputable musician make a careless observation that 'Ireland's *Sea Fever* is now so popular as to become a drawing-room ballad'. Clearly, an absurd proposition. But there is a disturbing element of truth in it. Style of performance can downgrade a simple art song in its effect, if the avowed aim is a performing success rather than poetic understanding. So let us endeavour to put forward unbiased definitions of both types. The drawing-room ballad depends upon an ability to use immediately attractive musical clichés to give expression to words which are not really profound in feeling; and to do so in a stereotyped form which is generally acceptable, whether it be stanzaical, verse and chorus, or simple ABA in construction; and it is implicit in its success that it should offer the singer every opportunity to exploit his prowess in some striking way. In other words, performance will

D

be more vocal than poetic, even if it gives the illusion of being emotional. Walter Ford's definition of art song (as quoted by Harry Plunket Greene in his *Interpretation in Song*, page 199) states that 'the music is not bounded by the stanza form of poetry, but forms a running commentary on its contents with a pictorial and emotional background, provided by the accompaniment'. Personally, I would like to reword it. The writing of an art song demands a skill in reconciling the differences between verbal and musical principles in such a way that voice and accompaniment can furnish the artistic concept of an organic musical form and a poetic whole. Here a word might be interposed about the current developments in the accompanist's art. Even the accompanist in the family drawing-room improved enough to encourage the song-writer to attempt something more adventurous and artistic than the perfunctory 'vamping' which had characterised so much of nineteenth-century song.

The impulse with which we are now concerned stems from the impress of German *Lieder* on all forms of solo song in the whole century, and from the influence of Parry and Stanford on English song particularly. And the work of the Edwardian and Georgian poets was also a notable influence.

The song cycle *Maud*, by Sir Arthur Somervell, is a work of considerable importance. As a one-time private pupil of Parry's he was, so to speak, a direct descendant of the Renaissance of 1880. His five song cycles include *A Shropshire Lad* (Housman), *Love in Springtime* and *A Broken Arc* (Browning). Undoubtedly *Maud* reveals a colourful and sensitive affinity with the Tennysonian muse, just as his *Shropshire Lad* offers a sensitive understanding of Housman. His separate songs, *Young love lies sleeping* and *Shepherd's Cradle Song* have a distinct place in the repertoire. Charles Wood must gain inclusion here for his superb *Ethiopia saluting the colours* and the album of ten songs for low voice now published by Boosey. Nor should we forget Benjamin Dale's *O Mistress Mine, Come away death* and *I heard a linnet* (Bridges) which are well up to the musical quality of his masterly choral work *Before the paling of the stars*.

Three widely different composers must concern us next: Bantock, Cyril Scott and Roger Quilter. The first-named was an astonishingly prolific song-writer.[1] One could hardly expect such a vast output to be equal in merit. It must be admitted that he has failed to maintain his one-time popularity, although he once enjoyed a considerable vogue. He wrote at least six volumes of *Songs of the East* to poems by his wife, Lady Bantock, a daughter of Hermann von Schweitzer. The oriental touches in these and other songs (culled, possibly, from his many tours abroad as examiner for the Trinity College of Music) are now regarded as rather synthetic and not really authentic. One feels it would have been better had he written less and revised more. While a few songs like *Lament of Isis*, *The March* (to a poem by J. C. Squire), *Feast of Lanterns* and *The Celestial Weaver* have survived, his creative inspiration was never very memorable, except in his excellent part-songs for male-voice choirs and a few major works like *Fifine at the Fair* (Birmingham, 1912), *Atlanta in Calydon* (Manchester, 1912) and *Vanity of Vanities* (Liverpool, 1914). His influence on and interest in the Competitive Music Festival movement was considerable. He was Professor of Music at Birmingham University, succeeding Elgar, from 1907 to 1934, and he was knighted in 1930. Cyril Scott, who was a fellow student with Quilter at Frankfort under Iwan Knorr, was a fairly prolific song-writer, though not to the same extent as Bantock, but like him he outlived his erstwhile popularity, though a little unfairly. Like Bantock, Scott had an interest in the Orient, but this arose from his pre-occupation with Oriental philosophy and theosophy. Although this brought a marked change of style to his music, it had little effect on his songs, despite an elaborate method of irregular barring and the omission of key signatures which he adopted for a time, e.g., *Sonata for violin and piano*. Arthur Jacob has rightly said that the 'latter-day neglect [of Scott's songs] is rather more astonishing than the supposedly exaggerated vogue which the composer once enjoyed'.[2] Of the quality and effectiveness of his song writing there can be no doubt—his affinity with the poems of Dowson is particularly interesting—but the undeserved label of 'the English Debussy' which was applied to him was most

[1] See the list in *Grove's Dictionary*, Vol. I, pp. 412–15.
[2] *A History of Song* (Hutchinson), p. 166.

unfortunate. It drew the wrong sort of attention to some of his mannerisms and a certain sameness of flavour in his work. He had a strong sense of classical form, which gave a structural firmness to all he wrote. Singers still retain an affection for him and there will always be a place in the repertoire for the *Arietta*, the suave grace of the *Lullaby*, the mischievous charm of *Don't come in Sir, please*, the deft *Blackbird's Song*, and the evocative *Songs of Old Cathay* as well as the *Two Songs without words*.

Roger Quilter is, in many ways, a very different character. Here is a composer who, 'endowed with a fresh distinctive melodic sense, and a fine taste in the choice and setting of words, has held his own without making concessions to the advancement of musical vocabulary' and is 'your *English* composer par excellence'.[1] His songs are always graceful, fluent and spontaneous and admirably placed for the voice; his poets range from the Elizabethans to Tennyson and beyond. His catalogue is a large and varied one. The Shakespeare groups and the Herrick songs, e.g., the set *To Julia*, have real distinction. His setting of Blake's *Dream Valley* is, I think, a masterpiece and *Now sleeps the crimson petal* a near one, the ending not entirely avoiding a conventional cliché. He deservedly won the active attention of singers of the calibre of Muriel Foster, Gervase Elwes, Mark Raphael and others, to give his songs the refined interpretations they demand.

Martin Shaw has a not-inconsiderable catalogue of songs, some of which are truly inspired. His melodic gift is at once natural and elegant and thoroughly vocal. The simplicity of his *I know a Bank* is quite haunting. He brings a sensitive poignancy to his setting of Poe's *Annabel Lee*, and the graphic narration of his *Wood Magic* is compelling. Armstrong Gibbs is a composer who excels in the sensitive treatment of words and music, and he has shown a particular affinity for the poetry of Walter de la Mare. His incidental music to Maeterlinck's *Betrothal* (Gaiety Theatre, 1921) won considerable public interest and his *Midsummer Madness*, a comedy-with-music by Clifford Bax, enjoyed a successful season at the Lyric, Hammersmith, in

[1] *Grove's Dictionary*, Vol. VII, p. 955.

July 1924, when Marie Tempest made her last stage appearance in a part which required singing. He has written well over a hundred songs, many of which still enjoy popular esteem, e.g., *Five Eyes, Nod, Silver, Ann's Cradle Song, On Duncton Hill, This is a sacred city, The Flooded Stream* and, of course, the stirring *Ballad of Semmerwater*. He is always able to provide a deft and expressive piano accompaniment to his fluent and well-proportioned vocal melodies. Among his larger-scale works, one must mention the cantatas *The Birth of Christ* (Hereford, 1930), and *The Highwayman*, and his children's opera *The Great Bell of Burley* (libretto by Nancy Bush). There is also his Symphony in E (performed Bournemouth, 1933). In 1934 he was awarded the Cobbett Gold Medal for chamber music and in 1939 a choral symphony *Odysseus* was performed by the Royal Choral Society.

Michael Head has the happy knack of maintaining a popular appeal without sacrificing the intrinsic quality of his writing. One of his most popular songs is *Sweet chance, that led my steps abroad*, and it must surely be accorded the merit of being a delightfully apt setting of W. H. Davies's poetry. It was a habit of his to set several poems by the same author within a short period, though not always with the intention of making a song-cycle. His own ability as a singer and pianist contributed distinctive qualities to his song writing, and in his later songs he makes a more positive use of the accompaniment to set and sustain the mood. His light and delicate touch shows every sign of maintaining its appeal for a long time, and songs like *A Blackbird singing, Foxgloves, October Valley, A Green Cornfield* and *The Singer* (unaccompanied) will certainly keep an assured place in the repertoire. The characteristic songs of Hamilton Harty deserve mention here, e.g., the dramatic *Sea Wrack*, the charming *Lane o' Thrushes, The Fiddler of Dooney* and *Come O come, my life's delight*. As might be expected from such a supreme accompanist, his piano parts are most effective.[1] There will be those who would also advance claims for the songs of van Someren-Godfrey and D. M. Stewart. The former may be a

---

[1] As a young singer, I once had the unexpected pleasure of singing to his accompaniment. It was an unforgettable event.

little fussy and involved but there is a certain merit in his settings of poems by A. C. Benson. But probably his settings of Humbert Wolfe's poems and his *Ozymandias* will attract singers more. Stewart may seem, for some tastes, to be somewhat stereotyped and a little too Parryesque, but his *Phantoms* and *The Cradle of the living God* have a lot of character. Frank Bridge, as a one-time pupil of Stanford and on the evidence of his exquisite chamber music and his refined *cantabile* writing, might have been expected to be a notable contributor to English song; but such expectations were not fully realised. However, his settings of Tagore, his *Go not happy day, O that it were so, Blow out you bugles* and *Love went a-riding* (despite the fantastically difficult accompaniment) must certainly be remembered.

To avoid straying into too many byways in our discussion, I have deliberately consigned to an appendix some publishers' selected lists of twentieth-century English song, for consultation. It may be noticed that nowadays publishers almost invariably include the names of the poets, a significant trait, indicative of the attention which the present-day singer gives to the words of a song. Plunket Greene's superb book, *Interpretation in Song*, has become a gospel to singers and singing teachers, and rightly so. But like so many good things, it can suffer from exaggeration. It is all too easy to take some of his splendid Rules and Principles out of context to justify applying them without due artistic discrimination, e.g., the singer's expressive pauses and rhythmic quirks. Interpretation can hardly justify too much interference with the musical facts, and to give the words *absolute* priority over the music can be dangerous. Logically, the composer will have interpreted the words himself, and it is with this interpretation that the singer will be concerned. And as to the question of word-painting, Harry Greene has himself uttered the warning 'Don't paint your details at the expense of your picture'. So, while it is right that the singer should make himself familiar with the poem before he starts the study of a song, it is also true that he must be able to appreciate the composer's own fusion of words and music in order to express the composite design. And it must never be forgotten that interpretation alone will not make up for, nor condone, technical or vocal shortcomings. These thoughts and their ancillary arguments will much concern us as we progress to the third stream of effort, that of the development of the modern type of English art song.

I do not wish to belabour this argument about interpretation too much, and I hope my remarks are not taken to mean more than they say. Of course words are important to the singer, but they are equally so to the composer. Compare, for example, the respective settings of *Sleep* by Warlock and Gurney. The singer will obviously be more concerned with the differences than with any similarities between the two songs, and not only with a detail like the different stress on 'O let *my* joys have some abiding' as compared with 'O let my *joys* have some abiding', indicative though it is of the respective characters of the composers. In short, it is always a question of words *and* music. Moreover, excessive pre-occupation with the simple clarity of diction can lead to a stilted syllabic enunciation, which undermines rather than underlines the musical intent.

We have reached a point when three distinguished composers claim our interest, though for different reasons; Ralph Vaughan Williams, Gustav Holst and Frederick Delius. The last-named is probably more important for the influence he exerted on some of our younger composers, like Warlock, Moeran and Orr, than for his actual contributions to English song. His three settings of Shelley's *Indian Love Song*, *Love's Philosophy* and *To the Queen of my heart*, were favoured items in the repertoire of the late Heddle Nash, who brought them to eloquent and impassioned performance. *Irmelin, Spring the sweet Spring* and *It was a Lover* are also notable songs; while *Cynara* (Dowson) and *A Late Lark* (Henley) are at their best with orchestral accompaniment. His most popular songs are undoubtedly *Twilight Fancies* and *Sweet Venevil* and these are modelled as closely on Grieg's original Björnson settings as Schubert's *Hagars Klage* was on Zumsteeg's. But it cannot be denied that the impress of 'Delian harmony' did bring something like a new dimension to English song, as we shall presently see. The close friendship of our other two composers is now well known through the book *Heirs and Rebels* published by Oxford University Press, and from it we can glean something of their critical approach to each other's work. It may be argued that the due appreciation of Holst's greatness as a composer was not as fully realised as it might have been in his own lifetime, but he is now slowly coming into his own. His radical mind was governed by an acute critical capacity and this, with his meticulous attention to technical problems, may make his music too intellectual for some tastes. However, there can be little excuse for singers ignoring his excellent settings of Humbert Wolfe's poems, all of which (there are a dozen published by Augener) I would roundly declare are masterpieces in English song. They compel close and careful study because some effects are implied, rather than conveyed; and they are as close a fusion between words and music as can be imagined. They were composed in 1929. Some of his earlier songs, like the *Six songs for baritone* (1902) containing *The Sergeant's Song*; and *The Heart Worships* (Buckton, 1907) did have quite a vogue at one time, and his *Four Songs for Voice and Violin* to medieval poems also attracted a good deal of attention for all their comparative austerity. Nor must we forget the striking *Hymns from the Rig Veda*.

The massive figure of Vaughan Williams stands astride the whole century. His earlier songs, like *Whither must I wander*, *The splendour falls*, *Claribel* and *Linden Lea* were written before the turn of the century, though not published until a decade later. The much loved *Songs of Travel* (Stevenson) were written before 1907 and were originally published in two sets of three and four songs, but now with the posthumous addition of *I have trod the upward and downward slope* are issued in one volume of eight songs and have much the feeling of a song-cycle. Eight of his *Nine Songs* by Housman for voice and violin are now published under the title *Along the Field*. Better known are his other Housman settings: *On Wenlock Edge*, for tenor voice and piano quintet, written in 1909. Because these songs were produced soon after the composer's sojourn in Paris as a pupil of Ravel, many have professed to see in them evidence of being 'frenchified'. I find not the slightest evidence of this. Similarly his active pre-occupation with English folk song is often cited as a notable influence on his songs, but Arthur Jacob is obviously right in regarding it 'less as a direct influence than as a catalyst'. In other words it is a liberating factor in his creative impulse but not a formative ingredient. *The House of Life*, settings of six sonnets by D. G. Rossetti was written in 1903 and contains the much loved *Silent Noon*, the success of which has distracted attention from the other items in the set, and at least two of them are well worth attention. His *Merciles Beauty*, a setting of three rondels by Chaucer for soprano solo and string trio, also deserves far more attention than it gets nowadays.

The *Four Hymns for tenor, piano and viola obbligato*, dedicated to Sir Stuart Wilson and first performed at Worcester in 1920, and the *Five Mystical Songs* to poems by George Herbert, are typical examples of the musical maturity the composer could bring to a style which he associates with religious words. Then there are his Shakespeare songs—he made two settings of *Orpheus with his lute*, and, of course, the remarkable settings of four poems by Fredegond Shove, in which one draws special attention to the graphic realism of *The New Ghost* and the colourful impressionism of *The Water Mill*, where we have the best example of the composer's piano writing and a vocal line which has all the sublime ease of spontaneous narrative.

The name of Ivor Gurney must have an honoured place in the ranks of English song writers, coupled with a gentle sorrow for the disappointments and delusions which clouded his somewhat unhappy life. The two Housman song cycles, *Ludlow and Teme* and *The Western Playland* were both published in 1924 and probably represent his finest work. In a way he recalls Campion in his rare combination of poet and musician, but his music is essentially classical in style and has many of the characteristics of Schubert. His sensitive melodic line is always poetically conceived with a subtle rhythmic pointing; and if his piano accompaniments are sometimes a little involved and thick, he could achieve something almost magical in this direction; e.g., *Last Hours*. Forty of his songs are now available in four volumes published by the Oxford University Press, but outside these quasi-memorial publications one must cite the immortal *Sleep*, the exquisite *Desire in Spring*, to words by Ledwidge, as well as the superlative *Severn Meadows* (to his own poetry), which would still carry his name to immortality even if all his other songs were lost. His was a rare spirit set in search for beauty but destined to be thrust into the turmoil of the world's ugliest war and being destroyed thereby. Another victim of the First World War was George Butterworth. His death in action was a grievous loss to English song. Though he destroyed so many of his manuscripts before he went to war, enough remained to justify the speculation of his being a great song writer. He shared with Vaughan Williams an active participation in the English folk-song revival, as witnessed by his many arrangements of folk songs. Apart from his Housman settings, in two sets, *A Shropshire Lad* and *Bredon Hill*, which are outstanding, I must confess to a strong liking for his *I fear thy kisses* (Shelley), *Requiescat* (Wylde) and *Love blows as the wind blows* (Henley). Yet another victim of the First World War was Denis Browne whose songs *Arabia*, *Diaphenia* and *To Gratiana* are sensitive and beautiful enough to show that his death was another tragic loss to English song. The character of Peter Warlock (the nom de plume of Philip Heseltine) is of a different stamp. Vigorous and wilful in spirit, his music is a curious admixture which stems from the positive influence of Delius and van Dieren, his own scholarly researches in Elizabethan music, and a creative impulse that was moody, vital and a little capricious. Yet no one can deny that he is a song writer of outstanding merit. The considerable variety in the style and mood of his songs makes it difficult to discuss them in a single paragraph.[1] In a list of violently contrasting styles, there are the bucolic, masculine items like *Captain Stratton's Fancy*, *Jillian of Berry*, *Good Ale* and many others. Then there are the more lyrical, quasi-Elizabethan songs like *Rest Sweet Nymphs*, *Sleep* and *As ever I saw*, and the love songs like *In an Arbour Green*, *The Contented Lover* and the simple charm of sets like the *Lilligay* cycle and the delicious *Candlelight*, settings of nursery rhymes. Certain significant points of technique are common to all his songs, the confident fluency and poise of the vocal line, the intriguing harmonic pungencies in his accompaniments and the meticulous attention he gives to the sense and enunciation of the words. I realise I should have named Bernard van Dieren

[1] See 'The Chronology of Warlock's Songs', K. Avery; *Music & Letters*, XXIX, 1948. 'Some notes on the songs of Peter Warlock', Gerald Cockshott, *Music & Letters*, XXI, 1940. *Peter Warlock: A Memoir*, Cecil Gray (1934).

some time ago. He had a certain vogue among the *avant garde* of his day and his wide literary knowledge enabled him to set French, German and English poetry with equal facility. His work never made much headway outside a small circle of friends and admirers and he seems now to be lost (perhaps a little unjustly) in a limbo betwixt the trenchant criticism of Blom ('tortuous and unvocal') and the hopelessly exaggerated praise of Cecil Gray. The songs of Arnold Bax are rather marred by his pre-occupation with the piano part, but there is a haunting sense of atmosphere in his *Seven Selected Songs* (including *The White Peace*) and the *Celtic Song Cycle*. Two other songs which are quite popular are *In the morning* and *I heard a piper*.

The significance of John Ireland in the history of English song can hardly be over-estimated. Though it would be a mistake to regard him as a miniaturist it is true he has written chiefly and most successfully in the more intimate and lyrical forms. Of the individuality of his musical idiom there can be no doubt and one must recognise also the rich and far-ranging resource of his harmonic technique. It is not difficult to find the customary 'three' periods in his creative activity. Up to 1920 we have the formative and more traditional aspects, though still highly individual; the subsequent decade was the most personal, productive and mature phase, while from 1940 onwards he gave more attention to larger works. But this is rather arbitrary in some ways. He developed an assured technique quite early on, and his venturesomeness is only matched by his absolute integrity. As a professor of composition at the Royal College of Music, he exercised a practical influence on several of his younger contemporaries such as Benjamin Britten, E. J. Moeran, Humphrey Searle and Richard Arnell. Peter Crossley-Holland, another pupil, has said: 'The significance of Ireland's songs and song cycles goes beyond the settings alone. The composer has in his selections from Housman (10 settings), Hardy (9 settings), D. G. Rossetti (5 settings) and many other poets played his part in liberating English song writing from the indifferent choice of words during the Victorian period. His choice is often ahead of that of the German *Lieder* writers, and in England he has in this respect few, if any, equals.'[1] He has equals but no superiors. His literary taste is understandable enough. Both his parents were well-known authors who died, unfortunately in straitened circumstances, while the composer was in his teens and only just beginning his musical training.

We can do little more here than glance at some of the highlights in his long and varied catalogue of song from the first song cycle *Songs of a Wayfarer*, written in the first decade of the century and dedicated to the singer Robert Radford, down to the *Five XVIth Century Poems* of 1941. But one must draw particular attention to his expressive settings of Housman; e.g., *The Land of Lost Content*; and I would roundly declare *The Lent Lily* to be one of his greatest songs. His *Songs Sacred and Profane* offers a cycle of exceptional range, both in emotion and ideas. A setting of a Harold Monro sonnet, *Earth's Call*, is also an outstanding dramatic essay, while *The Sacred Flame* (Mary Coleridge) with its interesting echoes of the symphonic poem *The Forgotten Rite*, is beautifully atmospheric in quality. It is not easy to explain why pianists should have taken more whole-heartedly to Ireland's lyricism than singers, who seem generally to be content with little more than a handful of the composer's more popular essays.

E. J. Moeran probably inherited his natural melodic gifts from his Irish father, a clergyman, and his own warm and active enthusiasm for folk song, particularly of his native Norfolk. His sensitive and colourful harmonic idiom owes much to his mentor, John Ireland, and his friendship with Delius and Warlock. If there were early signs that their harmonic influence at first engulfed his natural genius, once he had absorbed and made them subject to his strongly individual spirit he was able to turn to song writing with a distinct freshness of outlook and an engaging poetic instinct. His deeply felt Housman songs may show faint echoes of Butterworth, though with a deeper intensity perhaps, as is shown in the song cycle *Ludlow Town*. Not infrequently his deft rhythms have a freedom and gaiety which are quite infectious. The crowning achievement of his song writing reposes in the *Seven Poems by*

---

[1] *Grove's Dictionary*, Vol. IV, p. 537.

James Joyce (1927) and there are distinct marks of originality in the later *Four English Lyrics* (1933) and the *Four Shakespeare Songs* (1940); and no one would deny the endearing and indigenous qualities of the *Six Songs of Seumas O'Sullivan* (1944). The passing of the years has seen an increase in the popularity of his music possibly because, whether grave or gay, it has such integrity and charm.

Because there is always a touch of the exquisite in all Herbert Howells writes, I have often wished his output of songs had been greater or, at least, more positively recognised. Singers can be grateful indeed for what is provided although, sad to say, many of his earlier songs are not now easily available. Even the comparatively recent cycle *In Green Ways* seems to be out of print,[1] which is highly regrettable because all five songs are truly delightful. For me, *Under the greenwood tree*, *Merry Margaret* and *Wanderer's Nachtlied* are particularly so. In the meantime, songs like *Gavotte* (Newbolt), *A Madrigal* (Dobson), *O my deir hert* (Anon.) and the matchless *King David* continue to hold a favoured place in the repertoire. For their felicitous charm, Peterkin's dozen songs, including *I heard a piper*, *The garden of Bamboos*, *I wish and I wish*, and *A little wind came* are worth mentioning here. And although some of Elizabeth Poston's songs have vanished from the publishers' catalogues, one is glad that *Sweet Suffolk Owl* and *The Queen of Sheba's song* still remain.

A composer who merits a high place in the hierarchy of English song is C. W. Orr. He has concentrated his attention almost entirely on song writing and shows three distinct influences, his enthusiasm for Hugo Wolf, many of whose songs he has translated into eminently singable English; his friendship with Delius, and his unyielding admiration for Housman's poetry. I have always felt quite strongly that singers have been very neglectful of his songs and expressed myself so in an article as long ago as 1937.[2] Apart from his thoroughly sensitive Housman settings, he has a setting of *Silent Noon* which is not entirely overshadowed by Vaughan Williams, and his *Tryste*

[1] I understand that it is to be republished by Galliard Ltd.

[2] 'The Songs of C. W. Orr', Sydney Northcote, *Music & Letters*, Vol. XVIII, October 1937.

Noel (Louise Imogen Guiney), *Earl of Bristol's Farewell* (Digby) and *When as I wake* (Hanney) together with *Plucking the Rushes* (from the Chinese) are thoroughly attractive songs. The song cycle *From a Shropshire Lad* (1927-33), published by Chester, is perhaps his crowning achievement. It is high time for him to receive the responsive recognition due to his sensitive genius.

The place of Sir Arthur Bliss in English song may not be so easy to determine. He seems to have concentrated mainly on larger scale works, in opera, ballet, film music, orchestral music, brass band music, and so on, but the vitality, neatness and appositeness which characterises all he writes lends a positive distinction to his songs, such as the *Serenade* for baritone and orchestra, the song cycle *The Four Seasons* (1923), the *Seven American Poems* (1940) and the *Three Romantic Songs* (de la Mare, 1922), as well as *Madame Noy* (for soprano), two wordless songs *Rhapsody* and *Rout*; and *The Enchantress*,[1] a scena for contralto and orchestra. And I also like his setting of Hardy's *Fallow deer at the lonely house*, and his *Rich or poor* (W. H. Davies) for voice and piano.

Sir William Walton has composed very little for solo voice, but the three songs from *Facade*: *Daphne*, *Through Gilded Trelisses* and *Old Sir Faulk*, are utterly distinctive and characteristic. These he dedicated to Dora and Hubert Foss, which reminds me that Foss himself should be remembered for his *Seven Poems of Thomas Hardy* for baritone, male chorus and instrumental accompaniment. In addition, he has a few other items published which reveal a certain sensitivity for words, but his greatest contribution to English song was his practical contacts with young composers which enabled him, as head of the music department of the Oxford University Press, to pursue an enthusiastic policy of publishing solo song, which was thoroughly enterprising and of lasting value.

The winsome personality and undoubted creative skill of Gerald Finzi must concern us next. His gentle and sensitive music is rapidly gaining the esteem of perceptive musicians everywhere, and his importance in the progress of solo song is considerable. The settings of Hardy's poems, *A Young Man's*

---

[1] Originally written for Kathleen Ferrier, published by Novello.

Exhortation show a closer affinity to and understanding of this notoriously difficult poet, than any other composer has attained. If his music shows something of the influence of Parry and Vaughan Williams, it is also plain that in its comparatively unobtrusive way his is a thoroughly individual creative gift. The justly-famed solo cantata *Dies Natalis,* for soprano (or tenor) and strings, is singularly beautiful, as is the later *Farewell to Arms.* His accompaniments are subtly contrapuntal, but the musical texture, though closely knit, is beautifully clear. His vocal lines show a sensitive feeling for the 'sound-values as well as the meanings of words', and even when he uses quasi-recitative, it is always apposite and thoroughly vocal. The Shakespeare cycle *Let us garlands bring* is remarkably good. So, too, his *Earth and Air and Rain,* a series of settings of Hardy poems, including one of his most popular songs *Rollicum Rorum.* But popularity is not in the nature of his meditative and sensitive genius. Without a doubt, he is one of the great figures in contemporary English song.

And so we come at length to the last sector of our survey, which is largely dominated by the figure of Benjamin Britten. It is generally conceded that he is at his best under the stimulus of words; and it is probably true that he possesses something of the enterprise and confidence of a twentieth-century Purcell, with not a little of the old Master's 'Englishness'. He also owes much to the inspiration of a singer, Peter Pears. For their interpretative association not only increased Britten's sensitivity to words, but also gave a certain technical point and character to his *cantilena.* At first, his collaboration with Auden, in the cycle *On This Island* and the cantata *Our Hunting Fathers;* and his settings of Rimbaud's *Les Illuminations* (for high voice and strings) revealed a singularly clever, but rather unemotional style. But with maturity his emotions deepened and his innate sense of mood grew more reflective. The *Seven Sonnets of Michelangelo,* which owed much to Pears, brought a striking sense of the *florid* in song, and some outstanding details in expression. The *Holy Sonnets of John Donne, The Serenade* (for tenor, horn and strings), and the exceptionally fine *Charm of Lullabies,* witnessed a new mastery and maturity. There has never been any doubting his subtle response to mood and his

melodic invention has well merited the often applied epithets
of abundant and flexible. I confess that I cannot like the sophis-
ticated ingenuity of his folk song arrangements, and I feel there
are some passages in his music when sheer inventiveness takes
something from its intensity. But he has made an enormous
impact on English music generally and English song particularly.

Michael Tippett, an 'ardent Purcellian', shows traces of
Purcell's influence in the two song cycles *Boyhood's End* (W. H.
Hudson) and *The Heart's Assurance* (Sidney Keyes and Alun
Lewis). Tippett, is in many ways a remarkable genius, though
not always easy to comprehend. Though his creative impulse is
deeply felt, there is generally a strange abstract quality in his
music. Peter Evans, writing on Tippett's vocal music in the
Symposium on the composer's sixtieth birthday, says: 'Other
writers have shared the doubts about the torrents of notes that
support the vocal lines of the odd-numbered songs in the cycle
The Heart's Assurance. It is a paradox of Tippett's whole creative
output, musical and literary, that he is at once the master of
the simple but penetrating idea and incapable of viewing it out
of relationship to the complexities it provokes in the lively
mind. It is easy enough to imagine (or, indeed, to recompose)
the Tippett songs in question with their proliferating under-
growth of piano figuration trimmed to the tidily pastoral. But
we are at once presented with an entirely different work . . . no
longer braced by the heroically controlled tension that is
induced when the singer must assert each note as a significantly
timed articulation of the piano's endless stream of sound.'[1]
Some remarks of Scott Goddard are also worth quoting: 'By
studying the vocal works, there will be discovered two qualities,
one of mind, one of spirit, that are implicit in the treatment of
the words and, when once recognised, can be traced elsewhere.
They are subtlety and integrity. They appear to be inseparable
in him, the inner man's art coeval with his exterior life.'[2]

Lennox Berkeley's charm and elegance, as well as his vitality
and keen literary taste, are amply demonstrated in his *Four*

[1] *Symposium on Michael Tippett's 60th birthday*, ed. Ian Kemp
(Faber).
[2] *Grove's Dictionary*, Vol. VIII, p. 483.

Poems of St Theresa (for contralto and strings) and the *Five Songs* by Walter de la Mare. Despite rather obvious Continental influences, his lyricism carries all the marks of an authentic personality. Of his more recent song cycle, *Autumn Legacy*, Martin Cooper has written that the songs 'reveal the rich and complex sensibility that the composer plainly has difficulty in mastering'. His Tennyson setting succeeds better than those of Beddoes and Hopkins, but the whole cycle is certainly a thoroughly praiseworthy essay.

Geoffrey Bush writes exceedingly well for the voice. If he betrays some influences of Ireland, there is also a characteristic freshness and originality in his music. See his *Four Songs from Herrick's Hesperides*, *Three Elizabethan Songs*, *Three songs of Ben Jonson* and his many separate titles like *My true love hath my heart*, *There is a garden in her face* and *She hath an eye*. And one must comment on his excellent editorship of several eighteenth-century songs. Bruce Montgomery has devoted much of his energies to some outstanding choral works and extensive contributions to film music. His remarkable *Shakespeare Songs*, published in two sets of four songs each, merit a considerably wider recognition than they have received so far. He has been described as having the makings of a new Warlock and with a little encouragement could be induced to make really significant contributions to contemporary English song. I recall a singularly beautiful setting of *My true love hath my heart* which I saw in MS some years ago. Other composers who must be mentioned here are Benjamin Frankel for his excellent song cycle *The Aftermath* (for tenor, chamber orchestra and an off-stage trumpet); Howard Ferguson for his song cycle *The Discovery*; Alan Rawsthorne for his *Mediaeval Diptych*, three medieval poems offering contrasting portraits of the Virgin Mary and with an accompaniment for an orchestra with violins and violas omitted; Phyllis Tate, whose outstanding song is *The Falcon*; and some of the songs of the African-born John Joubert, on the evidence of his *Five Songs* op. 5, and *Two Invocations* op. 26, may yet make their mark. And if this book should prompt a resurgence of interest in English song (as I hope it will) perhaps the MS examples of such composers as Arnold Cooke, Arthur Oldham, Ivor Walsworth, Richard Arnell and Anthony

Hopkins—a diversity of talent indeed—might more easily gain due recognition by publication at least.

I realise only too well that the survey I have attempted is not easily contained within the covers of a single book. Probably each chapter would require its own monograph. But my main aim has been to 'state a case' for English song in general, and to find some sense of purpose in its gradual progress. I know I have been guilty of digressing into other aspects of vocal music, like opera and oratorio, here and there; as well as into some questions of singing technique. At times this was unavoidable and I hope was reasonably apposite. Doubtless there will be those who would have expected a chapter on 'the poets', especially in twentieth-century song; while some may have thought I made too little of the influence of, say, Sullivan and the subsequent musical comedy era on Edwardian song. And there may even be those who see in the current popular trend towards folk song a certain excitement and enthusiasm which I should have introduced in some way into my argument. But, for my part, it is only in the reputable performances of artists such as Pat Shuldham Shaw and his like that I find much excitement and the right sort of influence among young people interested in song. Other manifestations, frequently American-based, seem to have forged their links with the commercial pop song and, all too often, forged is the operative word. Others may have looked for some formal categorisation and definition of the several types of song over the centuries, but I felt that the art of song was a bit too elusive for such treatment, which would yield little in actual understanding. A song is better experienced than explained. Moreover, song by its very nature is more subject to the caprices of popular taste and fashion than almost any other aspect of music and yet, at its highest achievement, is ever seeking an artistic solution of the complex relationship of words and music.

Mr Martin Cooper has declared that this relationship 'has undergone a complete and drastic change since the beginning of the present century'; and in the rest of a thoughtful and cogent essay[1] contrasts what he terms the 'literary' song writing

[1] 'The World of Music', *Daily Telegraph*, 4 September 1965.

of Wolf and his immediate successors with the ideas of Schoenberg and others in the matter. His provocative last paragraph may be worth quoting in full: 'Stravinsky's syllabic settings of Old English and Latin texts have provided models for many composers who feel that the literary setting of texts, according to their sense, is, (in spite of Britten) no longer possible and even represents a kind of anti-musical activity. In fact, if literature exercised an undue dominance over music during the later part of the nineteenth century, music today has taken its revenge and assumed the position of the art to whose condition all the other arts aspire.'

It is probably true to say that the song writer tends to stand aloof from many of the current experiments in other forms of creative music. He cannot forego the claims of pure melody—not the sort of melody which looks like the shortest distance between two dissonances—and he must ever remember that the term vocal *tessitura* does not refer only to range but also to tone colour and quality. Our best song writers have generally paid due heed to these matters and few will deny that in twentieth-century song, both in quantity and quality, England is able to face the world with a certain pride and conviction. Unhappily, it has occurred at a time when the public response to song has been harshly undermined and the cult of the song-recital is so much weakened. The 'welfare state' having become so enamoured of mere entertainment, its cultural pursuits are all too easily governed by the strength and cynicism of blatant commercial interests. Even the mass media of radio and television have succumbed to the gimmick-ridden majority, for whom the words 'Song' and 'Singing' have strange connotations. Song is essentially a form of chamber music, intimate, intense and eloquent, perhaps even esoteric. It requires all possible support from those who are prepared to listen to, as well as look at, musical performance. It is not narrow patriotism alone which would plead with the B.B.C., with its recently established Music Programme, as well as the Third, to give a closer and more frequent attention to the claims of English song. They have promised as much for English choral works. And if music clubs and colleges throughout the kingdom could spare, say, one or two programmes annually for an English song recital, occasionally thinking of the composer and poet as the 'stars' and not only the singer, it is reasonable to suppose that a slightly more popular interest could be created, and the art of singing could be restored to its artistic worth. The glamour of orchestral and operatic performance is not to be denied but, just as few instrumentalists would be prepared to sacrifice entirely the *sonata* for the *concerto*, so singers would wish to keep a place for the personal and lyrical aspects of their art as positively as the dramatic. And is it too much to hope that some recording companies might spare a little from the gains of their pop records to cover the cost of issuing some LP records of selected groups of English songs? One regrets that this was not done much earlier when we could have had authentic recorded performances by certain singers who tended to identify themselves with particular composers, e.g., Plunket Greene with Stanford, Keith Falkner with Parry, Stuart Wilson and Gervase Elwes with Vaughan Williams, Anne Thursfield and Dorothy Silk with Armstrong Gibbs, George Parker with Martin Shaw and John Ireland, and so on. There are still many among our singers today who could, if they would, furnish almost as considered a specialisation for such a series of records and one feels sure that these would quickly win the interest of the multitudes of amateur singers who, if only in the competitive festival movement alone, are bravely doing much to keep alive the claims of their native song writers.

*Selected lists from the leading publishers
of Twentieth-Century English Song*

AUGENER LTD, 148 Charing Cross Road, London W.C.2.

AUSTIN, FREDERIC
Songs of Unrest:
 Margaret (Mallock)
 In City streets (Smith)
 The Sleepers (Davis)

BRIAN, HAVERGAL
 The Birds (Blake)
 The Land of Dreams (Blake)

BREWER, A. HERBERT
 For Your Delight: Gloucester
 Song Cycle:
  Taste away: Love's
  power: The happy
  heart: Lullaby: The
  Miller and his cat

BRIDGE, FRANK
 Day after day (Tagore)
 Dweller in my deathless
  dreams (Tagore)
 Journey's End (Wolfe)
 Speak to me (Tagore)

BUTTERWORTH, GEORGE
 Bredon Hill and other songs
  from A Shropshire Lad
  (Housman)
  Bredon Hill
  O fair enough
  When the lad
  On the idle hill of
   summer
  With rue my hear is laden

BUTTERWORTH GEORGE (*contd.*)
 Six Songs from A Shropshire
 Lad:
  Loveliest of Trees
  When I was one and
   twenty
  Look not in my eyes
  Think no more lad
  The lads in their
   hundreds
  Is my team ploughing?
 I fear thy kisses (Shelley)

CAMPBELL, C. M.
 I saw thee weep (Byron)
 Love's Philosophy (Shelley)
 Time and Tide (Allen)

CARVER, DAVID
 When I go out to meet my
  love (Ould)

CRIPPS, A. R.
 Nine songs from A Shrop-
  shire Lad (Housman)
  O see how thick
  It nods and curtsies
  Is my team ploughing
  Into my heart
  Far in a western
   brookland
  On the idle hill of
   summer
  Think no more lad

CRIPPS, A. R. (*contd.*)
  Nine songs from a Shropshire
    Lad (Housman) (*contd.*)
      The lads in their
        hundreds
    Christmas Lullaby (Graves)
    Safety (Brooke)
    The Soldier (Brooke)

DELIUS, FREDERICK
  Longing (Grist)
  Slumber song (Grist)
  Summer Eve (Grist)
  Sunset (Grist)
  The Nightingale (Grist)
  In Eng. and German

DUNHILL, THOMAS F.
  Countryside Ditties
    The Shepherd (Blake)
    The lost Doll (Kingsley)
    Dainty little Maiden
      (Tennyson)
    The haymaker's
      roundelay (Anon)

FRANKEL, BENJAMIN
  The Aftermath (Nicholls)
  Song cycle for tenor, chamber
  orch., trumpet (interna.)

FRASER, NORMAN
  A sea dirge (Shakespeare)

HARRISON, SIDNEY
  When I set out for Lyonesse
    (Hardy)

HARTY, HAMILTON
  Rose Madness (Bultitaft)
  The Devon Maid (Keats)

HOLST, GUSTAV
  Twelve songs by Humbert
    Wolfe
      A little Music
      Betelgeuse

HOLST, GUSTAV (*contd.*)
  Twelve songs by Humbert
    Wolfe (*contd.*)
      Envoi
      In the street of lost
        time
      Journey's End
      Now in these fairy lands
      Persephone
      Rhyme
      The Dream City
      The floral bandit
      The Thought
      Things lovelier

IRELAND, JOHN
  The Land of Lost Content.
    Six songs by Housman
      The Lent Lily: Lads-
        love: Goal and
        wicket: The vain
        Desire: The En-
        counter: Epilogue
  Friendship in misfortune
    (Anon)
  Great things (Hardy)
  Love and friendship (Bronte)
  My true love hath my heart
    (Sir P. Sidney)
  Santa Chiara (Symons)
  Sea Fever (Masefield)
  The bells of San Marie
    (Masefield)
  The One Hope (Rossetti)
  The Trellis (Huxley)
  Vagabond (Masefield)

MILFORD, ROBIN
  Four seasonable songs
    Reeds of innocence
      (Blake)
    Pleasure it is (Cornyshe)
    Late Leaves (Landor)
    This endris night (Anon)

MOERAN, E. J.
Rosefrail (Joyce)
The sweet o' the year
(Shakespeare)

PARRY, SIR C. H. H.
Three Odes of Anacreon
(Moore)
Away you men of rules
Fill me as deep a draught
Golden hues of life are
fled

RUBBRA, EDMUND
In dark weather (Webb)

STANFORD, SIR C. V.
A Corsican Dirge (Strettell)
A message to Phyllis
(Heywood)
Crossing the bar (Tennyson)
La Belle Dame sans merci
(Keats)
May's love (Browning)
Prospice (Browning)
The Lute Song (Tennyson)
Milkmaid's Song (Tennyson)

STEWART, D. M.
A lawsuit (A. C. Benson)
A mystical song (C. Mon-
tague)
After lunch. *The words
translated from the Chinese
by A. Waley*
At the window (Tennyson)
Beauty the Pilgrim
(G. Gould)
Denny's daughter
(M. O'Neill)
Exultate Deo (L. Wilson)
Forest music (A. C. Benson)
Gone (Tennyson)
Hey nonny no! (Anon)
House of mine (Stevenson)

STEWART, D. M. (*contd.*)
Katrina's Sundial (H. Van
Dyke)
Love's precinct (A. C. Benson)
Night (Swinburne)
No answer (Tennyson)
Our Nell (H. Prince)
Phantoms (V. D. Goodwin)
Plucking the rushes. *The words
translated from the Chinese by
A. Waley*
Rising storm
(H. W. Burnaby)
Shells (C. Amory)
The cradle of the living God
(R. L. Gales)
The Great Orme (Tim)
The morning moon
(E. Bridges)
The self-unseeing (Hardy).
With violin obbligato
The stranger (W. de la Mare)
The tomb of Ajax
(A. C. Benson)
The trio (A. C. Benson)
The well (A. C. Benson)
The west wind (J. Masefield)
Through the fields in
summer (E. Shaldon)
Unchanging love
(A. C. Benson)
When (Tennyson)

VAN SOMEREN-GODFREY, M.
A little fete. *Words from the
poem from the Chinese of
Li-Tai-Po by Ian Colvin*
Anacreon. *Words from the
Greek Antipater, translated
by Humbert Wolfe*
Biton to his Gods. *Words
from 'Others Abide', by
Humbert Wolfe*

VAN SOMEREN-GODFREY, M.
(*contd.*)
Six Blake Songs:
Joy is my name: Piping
down the valleys: The
Shepherd: A Cradle
Song: Love's Secret:
A Poison Apple
Death, thy servant
(Rabindranath Tagore)
Four Songs:
The poems by Humbert
Wolfe. Green
Candles: Love and
Peter: Lamon to
Priapus; Journey's End
Go, teach the swan to swim
(E. N. da C. Andrade)
Ozymandias (Shelley)
La belle dame sans merci.
(Keats)
The day is no more
(Rabindranath Tagore)
The king of China's
daughter (E. Sitwell)
The old nurse's song
(E. Sitwell)
The Parting (Ian Colvin)
The tears of St Joseph (Ruth
Rogers)
The Twa Corbies
(Traditional Scots)
The white dress. Words by
Humbert Wolfe
Thou art not fair (Thomas
Campion)
Three Songs:
Shadow and Smoke: The
House on Fire: Night
Piece
*The poems by E. N. da C.
Andrade*
D*

SWAIN, FREDA
Experience. *Translated from
the Chinese by A. Waley*
Winter field (A. E. Coppard)

WARLOCK, PETER
Candlelight. A cycle of
nursery jingles:
How many miles to
Babylon?: I won't be
my father's Jack:
Robin and Richard:
O my kitten: Little
Tommy Tucker:
There was an old
man: I had a little
pony: Little Jack
Jingle: There was a
man of Thessaly:
Suky, you shall be my
wife: There was an
old woman: Arthur
O'Bower
Captain Stratton's fancy
(J. Masefield)
Eloré lo (Anon. 17th century)
Good ale (Anon. 15th century)
Hey, troly loly lo (Anon.
16th century)
Late summer (E. Shanks)
Mr Belloc's fancy (J. C.
Squire)
Piggesnie (Anon. 16th
century)
The bachelor (Anon. 15th
century)
The contented lover
(J. Mabbe. 1631)
The cricketers of Hambledon.
*Song with chorus. Words
B. Blunt.*
The droll lover (Anon. 17th
century)

WARLOCK, PETER (*contd.*)
The singer (E. Shanks)
To the memory of a great
singer (Stevenson)
Tom Tyler (Anon. 16th
century)

WARNER, H. WALDO
A parting (F. Haydn)
Flowers, awake (O. Frampton)
Heart of mine. Venetian
serenade (O. Frampton)

WARNER, H. WALDO (*contd.*)
The scent of the gorse
(J. A. McDonald)
WESTRUP, SIR JACK
Three Shakespeare Songs:
Come away Death
Take O take those lips
away
Orpheus with his lute
WHITE, FELIX
Harvest Home (Evans)
WHITE, MAUDE V.
When love began (Symonds)

BOOSEY & HAWKES, 295 *Regent Street, London W.1.*

BENJAMIN, ARTHUR
Jamaicalypso (Lewis)
Jan
Linstead Market
Song of the banana carriers
Wind's work (Moore)

BERKELEY, LENNOX
How love came in (Herrick)

BESLY, MAURICE
Columbine's garden
(Dowden)
Music when soft voices die
(Shelley)
My love goes with you
(Dowden)
Song in Loneliness
The second minuet (Dowden)

BLISS, SIR ARTHUR
Seven American poems. *For
low voice and piano.*

BRIDGE, FRANK
Come to me in my dreams
(Arnold)
E'en as a lovely flower (after
Heine)

BRIDGE, FRANK (*contd.*)
Go not happy day
(Tennyson)
Love went a-riding
(Coleridge)
The violets blue (after Heine)

BRITTEN, BENJAMIN
Fish in the unruffled lakes
(Auden)
Now thro' nights caressing
grip (Auden)
The Birds (Belloc)
A Charm of Lullabies. *Mezzo
soprano and piano*
Canticle I (Quarles).
High voice and piano.
Canticle II. *Alto, tenor
and piano.*
Canticle III. (Sitwell).
Tenor, horn and piano.
On this island (Auden)
Seven Sonnets of Michelangelo. *Tenor and piano.*
Songs from the Chinese. *High
voice and guitar.*
The holy sonnets of John
Donne. *High voice and piano.*

BRITTEN, BENJAMIN (*contd.*)
Winter words (Hardy). *High voice and piano.*

DELIUS, FREDERICK
A late lark (Henley)
Autumn (Jacobsen)
Cynara (Dowson)
In the garden of the seraglio (Jacobsen)
Irmelin (Jacobsen)
It was a lover and his lass (Shakespeare)
Silken shoes (Jacobsen)
So white, so soft, so sweet is she (Jonson)
Spring, the sweet spring (Nashe)
The violet (Holstein)
To daffodils (Herrick)

ELGAR, EDWARD
After (Marston)
In the dawn (Benson)
Is she not passing fair (*trans.* Costello)
Land of hope and glory (Benson)
Sea slumber song (Noel)
Song of liberty (Herbert)
Speak, music (Benson)
Where corals lie (Garnett)

FERRERS, HERBERT
Roister doister (Udall)

FINZI, GERALD
Budmouth dears (Hardy)
Come away, come away, death (Shakespeare)
Ditty (Hardy)
Her temple (Hardy)
O mistress mine (Shakespeare)
Rollicum-rorum (Hardy)
The sigh (Hardy)

FINZI, GERALD (*contd.*)
A young man's exhortation (Hardy). *For tenor and piano*
Before and after summer (Hardy). *For baritone and piano*
Earth and air and rain (Hardy). *For baritone and piano*
I said to love (Hardy). *For low voice and piano*
Let us garlands bring (Shakespeare). *For voice and piano*
Music for *Love's labour's lost* (Shakespeare). *For voice and piano*
Till earth outwears (Hardy). *For high voice and piano*

FRASER, NORMAN
Echo's lament (Jonson)
From the Brazilian (Meireles)
From the Chinese (Sheng)
From the Greek (Symonds)
Little Irish song (Beresford)
The snowdrop in the wind

GIBBS, C. ARMSTRONG
A song of shadows (de la Mare)
As I lay in the early sun (Shanks)
February (Currie)
Five Eyes (de la Mare)
Gone is my love (Harrhy)
Immortality (Currie)
Maritime invocation (Boyd)
Midnight (Lang)
Nod (de la Mare)
Sailing homeward (Sheng)
Silver (de la Mare)
Sweet sounds (de la Mare)
The fields are full (Shanks)
The hawthorn tree (Maude)

GIBBS, C. ARMSTRONG *(contd.)*
The Oxen (Hardy)
The summer palace (Ellis)
To Anise (Downes-Currie)
Why do I love ('Ephelia')
Joan of Arc. *For soprano and piano*

GURNEY, IVOR
Carol of the Skiddaw Yowes (Casson)
Come O come my life's delight (Campion)
Sleep (Fletcher)
Spring (Nashe)
Tears (Fletcher)
Under the greenwood tree (Shakespeare)

HARRISON, JULIUS
A Cavalier to his lady (Strode)
Boot, saddle, to horse (Browning)
Marching along (Browning)
Memory island (Askew)

HARTY, SIR HAMILTON
Bonfires (Bultitaft)
By the bivouacs fitful flame (Whitmans)
Come O come my life's delight (Campion)
Denny's daughter (O'Neill)
Lane O' the thrushes (O'Byrne and Healy)
Sea Wrack (O'Neill)
The fiddler of Dooney (Yeats)

HEAD, MICHAEL
A blackbird singing (Ledwidge)
A dog's life (Smith)
A funny fellow (Sherman)
A green cornfield (Rossetti)

HEAD, MICHAEL *(contd.)*
A Piper (with Flute Oboe) (O'Sullivan)
A sea burthen (Smith)
A slumber song of the Madonna (Noyes)
A vagabond song (Drinkwater)
Claribel (Tennyson)
Come take your lute (Taylor)
Constancy (Pitter)
Cotswold love (Drinkwater)
Foxgloves (Webb)
Gaiete and orior (Miller)
Green rain (Webb)
Had I a golden pound (Ledwidge)
Lean out of the window (Joyce)
Limehouse Reach (Smith)
Ludlow town (Housman)
Mamble (Drinkwater)
Money O (Devies)
O to be in England (Browning)
October valley (Bush)
On the wings of the wind (Miller)
Sancta et immaculata virginitas *(trans.* Bush)
Small Christmas tree (Gould)
Star candles (Rose)
Sweet chance that led my steps (Davies)
Sweethearts and wives (Smith)
The comet (Pitter)
The dreaming lake (Moore)
The estuary (Pitter)
The fairies' dance (Sherman)
The fairy tailor (Fyleman)

HEAD. MICHAEL (*contd.*)
The King of China's
daughter (Sitwell)
The little road to Bethlehem
(Rose)
The Lord's prayer
The robin's carol (Strong)
The ships of Arcady
(Ledwidge)
The singer *unaccompanied*
(Taylor)
The three mummers (Taylor)
The twins (Leigh)
The viper (Pitter)
The woodpath in spring
(Pitter)
There's many will love a
maid (Ross)
What Christmas means to
me (Lane)
When I came forth this
morn (Davies)
When sweet Ann sings (Rose)
Why have you stolen my
delight (Young)
You cannot dream things
lovelier (Wolfe)
You shall not go a-maying
(Currie)

HOWELLS, DR HERBERT
A Madrigal (Dobson)
King David (de la Mare)

HUGHES, HERBERT
O men from the fields
(Colum)

IRELAND, JOHN
A report song (Breton)
A thanksgiving (Bassus)
All in a garden green
(Howell)
An aside (*from* Harleian
MS 7578)

IRELAND, JOHN (*contd.*)
Blind (Cooper)
The cost (Cooper)
Hawthorn time (Housman)
I have twelve oxen (early
English)
If there were dreams to sell
(Beddoes)
Love is a sickness full of
woes (Daniel)
Spring sorrow (Brooke)
The heart's desire (Housman)
The holy Boy (Brown)
The soldier (Brooke)
Songs of a wayfarer. *For
voice and piano*

KEEL, FREDERICK
The merry month of May
(Dekker)
Trade winds (Masefield)
Three salt water ballads
(Masefield). *For voice and
piano*

MOERAN, E. J.
Rosaline (Lodge)

POSTON, ELIZABETH
Sweet Suffolk Owl (Vautor)

QUILTER, ROGER
Five Jacobean lyrics. *For high
or low voice and piano*
Five Shakespeare songs. *For
high or low voice and piano*
Four Shakespeare songs. *For
low voice and piano*
Seven Elizabethan lyrics. *For
low voice and piano*
Three Shakespeare songs. *For
medium or low voice and piano*
Amaryllis at the fountain
(Anon. 16th century)
An old carol (Anon. 15th
century)

QUILTER, ROGER (*contd.*)
Blow, blow, thou winter
wind (Shakespeare)
Come unto these yellow
sands (Shakespeare)
Cuckoo song (Williams)
Dream valley (Blake)
Fair house of joy (Anon.)
Fill a glass with golden wine
(Henley)
Hark! hark! the lark
(Shakespeare)
June (Hopper)
Love's philosophy (Shelley)
Non nobis, Domine (Kipling)
Now sleeps the crimson petal
(Tennyson)
O mistress mine (Shakespeare)
Tell me where is fancy bred
(Shakespeare)
The fuchsia tree
The jealous lover (Rochester)
The maiden blush (Herrick)
To daisies (Herrick)
When icicles hang by the
wall (Shakespeare)
Who is Silvia (Shakespeare)

SOMERVELL, SIR ARTHUR
Fain would I change that
note (Anon.)
Go not happy day
(Tennyson)
The street sounds to the
soldier's tread (Housman)
Young love lies sleeping
(Rossetti)
A Shropshire Lad. Song
cycle
Maud (Tennyson). A Song
cycle

STANFORD, SIR CHARLES
Boat Song (Pollock)

STANFORD, SIR CHARLES (*contd.*)
Drake's Drum (Newbolt)
I'll rock you to rest (Graves)
Johneen (O'Neill)
The calico dress (Jessop)
The fairy lough (O'Neill)
The old superb (Newbolt)
There's a bower of roses
(Moore)
An Irish Idyll in six minia-
tures (O'Neill). *For low
voice and piano*

VAUGHAN WILLIAMS, DR RALPH
Bright is the ring of words
(Stevenson)
I have trod the upward and
the downward slope
(Stevenson)
Is my team ploughing?
(Housman)
Linden lea (Barnes)
The roadside fire (Stevenson)
The sky above the roof
(Dearmer)
The splendour falls
(Tennyson)
The vagabond (Stevenson)
Whither must I wander
(Stevenson)
Four Hymns. *For tenor, viola
and piano*
On Wenlock Edge. *For tenor,
piano and string quartet ad
lib*
Songs of Travel (Stevenson).
For low voice and piano

WARLOCK, PETER
As ever I saw (Anon.)
Love for love (Anon.)
Mourn no more (Fletcher)
Sweet content (Dekker)
The countryman (Chalkhill)

WARLOCK, PETER (*contd.*)
The first mercy (Blunt)
The jolly shepherd
An album of Songs

WHITE, MAUD VALERIE
To Mary (Shelley)

WOOD, CHARLES
Ethiopia saluting the colours
(Whitman)

O captain, my captain
(Whitman)
The dead at Clonmacnois
(Rolleston)
Ten Songs. *For low voice and piano*

J. & W. CHESTER LTD, 11 Great Marlborough Street, London W.1

BANTOCK, SIR GRANVILLE
Easter Humn
Five songs from the Chinese
Set I:
The old fisherman
The Ghost Road
Under the Moon
The Celestial Weaver
Return of Spring
Five songs from the Chinese
Set II:
The tomb of Chao-Chun
A dream of Spring
Desolation
The island of Pines
The pavilion of abound-
ing joy
The Marsh (J. C. Squire)
Salve Regina

BAX, SIR ARNOLD
Album of seven selected
songs:
A Milking Sian
Christmas Carol
The enchanted fiddle
Roundel
Shieling Song
To Eire
The White Peace
A Celtic Song-cycle:
Eilidh my Fawn

BAX, SIR ARNOLD (*contd.*)
A Celtic song cycle (*contd.*)
Closing doors
Thy dark eyes to mine
A Celtic Lullaby
At the last
The Fairies
Golden Gwendolin
Magnificat
O dear what can the matter
be
I have a house and land in
Kent

BEDFORD, HERBERT
Homecoming
The heart has chambers
twain
To a water lily
Night piece

BERKELEY, LENNOX
The Beacon Barn
Bells of Cordoba
Five songs (de la Mare):
The horseman
Poor Henry
Mistletoe,
Song of the soldier
Silver
Three Greek Songs:
Four Poems of
St Teresa

BERKELEY, LENNOX (*contd.*)
Three Greek songs (*contd.*)
Five poems
(W. H. Auden)
Ode de premier jour
de Mai
Autumn's Legacy. Song cycle

BLISS, SIR ARTHUR
Madame Noy. *For soprano*
The Women of Yueh. Five
songs by Li-Po

GOOSSENS, SIR EUGENE
Persian Idylls
Afternoon
Epigram
Tea-time
The Curse
The appeal
Melancholy
Philomel
Four Songs:
Threshold
A Winter-night Idyll
A woodland dell
Seascape

HOLBROOKE, J.
Marino Faliero (Byron)
Scena for bass and
orchestra

HOLST, GUSTAV
Op. 24, Vedic Hymns for
Solo Voice
First Group: 1, Ushas
(Dawn): 2, Varuna I
(Sky): 3, Maruts
(Stormclouds).
Medium
Second Group: 4, Indra
(God of Storm and
Battle): 5, Varuna II
(The Waters): 6, Song
of the Frogs. *Medium*

HOLST, GUSTAV (*contd.*)
Third Group: 7, Vac
(Speech): 8, Creation:
9, Faith. *Medium*
Op. 35, Four Songs for
Voice and Violin:
1, Jesu Sweet, now will
I sing: 2, My Soul
has Naught but Fire:
3, I sing of a Maiden:
4, My Leman is so
True. *Medium*

HOPKINS, ANTONY
Humble song to the birds. *A
cantata for high voice*
A melancholy song
Nocturne (Four Tudor
Sonnets)

IRELAND, JOHN
The Adoration
The Rat
Rest

JACOBSON, M.
Still Life (Nature Morte)

LAMBERT, CONSTANT
Three poems by Li-Po:
The ruin of the Ku-su
Palace
The intruder
On the city street

LE FLEMING, C.
Egypt's might is tumbled
down
God be in my head
If it's ever spring again
In a sleepless night
The Hills of Heaven
To an isle in the water

MOERAN, E. J.
The bean flower (March)

ORR, C. W.
  Plucking the Rushes. *Medium*
  Seven Songs from 'A Shrop-
    shire Lad':
      1, Along the Field: 2,
      When I Watch the
      Living Meet: 3, The
      Lent Lily: 4, Farewell
      to Barn: 5, Oh Fair
      Enough: 6, Hughley
      Steeple: 7, When
      Smoke Stood Up.
      Baritone
  Silent Noon. *Medium*
  The Carpenter's Son. *High*
  Three Songs from 'A Shrop-
    shire Lad':
      1, Into my heart an air
      that kills: 2, Westward
      on the high-hilled
      plains: 3, Oh see how
      thick the goldcup
      flowers. *Tenor*
  The Isle of Portland. *Baritone*
  Two Songs from 'A Shrop-
    shire Lad':
      1, 'Tis time I think by
      Wenlock Town: 2,
      Loveliest of trees, the
      Cherry. *Medium*
  When I was one and
    twenty. *High*

ORR, C. W. (*contd.*)
  When the lad for longing
    sighs. *High*

WARLOCK, PETER
  Peterisms, Set I:
      1, Chopcherry: 2, A Sad
      Song: 3, Rutterkin.
      High
  Lilligay, Five Songs:
      1, The Distracted Maid:
      2, Johnny wi' the tye:
      3, The Shoemaker: 4,
      Burd Ellen and
      Young Tamlane: 5,
      Rantum Tantum. *High*
  Saudades, Three Songs:
      1, Along the Stream: 2,
      Take O take those
      lips away; 3, Hera-
      cleitus

WHYTE, IAN
  She dwelt amongst the
    untrodden ways. *Low*
  Piping down the valleys
    wild. *Medium*
  The sun has long been set.
    Medium
  Wine of the Fairies. *Medium*
  Twilight. *Medium*

J. B. CRAMER & CO, 139 New Bond Street, London W.1.

BAINTON, EDGAR
  To the children

BANTOCK, SIR GRANVILLE
  And there are tears
  Bird of St Bride
  By the rivers of Babylon
  Court of Dreams
  Dancing

BANTOCK, SIR GRANVILLE
  (*contd.*)
  Fireside Fancies
  Great is the Lord
  The Lost One
  Memories with the dusk
    return
  Morgan le Fay

BANTOCK, SIR GRANVILLE
(*contd.*)
Night on the mountain
Nocturne
Out of the depths
Robin redbreast
Singer in the wood
Song to the seals
Spring song
The valley of silence
Youthful Charming Chloe

DUNHILL, THOMAS
April
Evening
Gifts
Go pretty birds
The holy babe
I can hear a cuckoo
If ever I marry at all
If I'd been Mrs Noah
I remember
I think of you (*Tantivy Towers*)
Little town of Bethlehem
Quiet Night, The
The Suffolk Owl
Sweet July
Three kings of Somerset
Visit from the Moon
FOSS, HUBERT
Winter Chant

HARRISON, SIDNEY
Fairy Tales
I hear an army

HOLBROOKE, JOSEF
Killary

IRELAND, JOHN
Her song
Summer schemes
Weathers
E

KEEL, FREDERICK
Bee's song
Bonny George Campbell
Christmas Carol
Escape at bedtime
I loved a lass
Mocking fairy
Music when soft voices die
Nocturne
Remembrance
Sea burthen
Sergeant's song
Ship of Rio
Song of the thrush
There sits a bird on yonder tree
Twilight
When icicles hang by the wall

MOREAN, E. J.
Day of Palms

O'NEILL, NORMAN
The golden hour of noon
Home of mine
I have a flaunting air
May lilies
Musette
On a grey day
When May walks by

PEEL, GRAHAM
Ferry me across the water
Go down to Kew in lilac time
Lute Player, The
Nick Spence
The wild swan

SHAW, MARTIN
The accursed wood
Annabel Lee
At Columbine's grave

Messrs J. CURWEN & SONS LTD, 29 Maiden Lane, London W.C.2.

AUSTIN, FREDERIC
The Sayler's song (*Trad.*)

BENJAMIN, ARTHUR
Before Dawn (de la Mare)
Calm Sea and Mist (Sharp)
Diaphenia (Constable)
Hey nonny no (Anon.)
The Mouse (McCrae)
The Wasp (Sharp)

BESLY, MAURICE
An Epitaph (de la Mare)
Listening (H.H.)

BLISS, SIR ARTHUR
The Buckle (de la Mare)
A Child's Prayer (Sassoon)
Fallow deer at the lonely
house (Hardy)
The Hare (de la Mare)
Rich or Poor (Davies)
Three Romantic Songs (de
la Mare)

BONTOFT, FREDERIC
All that's past (de la Mare)

BOUGHTON, RUTLAND
Foam Song (M. Agrell)
Holiness (John Drinkwater)
Immanence (J. Rodker)
Love of Comrades, The
(Walt Whitman)
Lullay (Traditional)
Sweet Ass (E. Farjeon)
Symbol Songs (Poems by
Mary Richardson)
Blue in the Woods
Mother Mary

BROOK, HARRY
At Michael's Gate (Kingsley)
Little One Hush (Haskins)

BROWN, H
Ha'nacker Mill (H. Belloc)

BRUCE, M. CAMPBELL
The Rain (Davies)
Snow (de la Mare)

DUNHILL, THOMAS F.
To the Queen of Heaven
(Anon.)

GIBBS, C. ARMSTRONG
Ballad of Semmerwater
(Watson)
The Birch Tree (Mase)
The Cherry Tree (Rose)
Danger (Currie)
The Exile (de la Mare)
The Flooded Stream
(Cropper)
The Galliass (de la Mare)
The Mad Prince (de la Mare)
Mistletoe (de la Mare)
Nightfall (Dawson)
On Duncton Hill (Grant)
Orchard sings to the child
(Cropper)
Proud Maisie (Scott)
Resting (Grant)
Songs from *Croaaings*
(de la Mare):
Araby
Ann's Cradle song
Beggar's Song
Songs from *Midsummer
Madness* (Bax):
Chains of love
Neglected Moon
Summer Night (Agrell)
Take Heed young heart
(de la Mare)
This is a sacred city
(Masefield)
Tiger Lily (Bouverie)
To one who passed whistling
thro' the night (Agrell)

GIBBS, C. ARMSTRONG (*contd.*)
Wanderer (de la Mare)
When I was one and twenty
(Housman)

GOOSENS, SIR EUGENE
When thou art dead (from
The Constant Nymph)

HART, FRITZ
Refuge (A. E.)

HAY, NORMAN
Buttermilk Boy (*Trad.*)
Churnin' Day (Shane)
Tryste Noel

HOLLAND, THEODORE
Song of Lamentation

HOWELLS, HERBERT
Peacock Pie Set 1 (de la
Mare)

HURLSTONE, WILLIAM Y.
Dry those fair, those crystal
eyes (King)
That time is dead (Shelley)

IRELAND, JOHN
Bed in Summer (Stevenson)

JACOBSON, MAURICE
Boys (Letts)
Jolly good ale and old
(Stevenson)
Queen Mab (Hood)
The Roman Road (Laing)
Savoury Seal (Parry)

MOERAN, E. J.
Blue-eyed Spring (Nicholls)
Loveliest of Trees (Housman)
Spring goeth all in white
(Bridges)
When June is come (Bridges)

PARKER, CLIFTON
My Father's Close (Rossetti)

PLUMSTEAD, MARY
Down by the Salley Gardens
(Yeats)
Grey Wind, The (Wain-
wright)
Sigh no more
Take O take those lips away

QUILTER, ROGER
Cradle in Bethlehem, The
(Bennett)
Music (Shelley)
Music and Moonlight
(Shelley)
One word is too often
profaned (Shelley)

RAFTER, LEONARD
The Huxter (Thomas)

ROOTHAM, CYRIL
A Child's Prayer (Sassoon)

ROSS, COLIN
The Cherry hung with snow
(Housman)

RUBBRA, EDMUND
Take O take those lips away
Why so pale and wan?

SHAW, MARTIN
Brookland Road (Kipling)
Cuckoo (*Trad.*)
Down by the Salley Gardens
(Yeats)
Easter Carol (Rossetti)
Egg-Shell, The (Kipling)
Heffle Cuckoo Fair (Kipling)
Invictus (Henley)
Love Pagan (Cripps)
Make we merry (*Trad.*)
Oh, Falmouth is a fine town
(Henley)
Old Mother Laid-in-wool
(Kipling)
Over the Sea (Rossetti)

SHAW, MARTIN (*contd.*)
  Pity Poor Fighting Men
    (Kipling)
  Serenade (Gardner)
  Song of the Palanquin
    Bearers (Naidu)
  Summer (Rossetti)
  When daisies pied (Shakespeare)
SWAIN, FREDA
  Blessing (Clarke)
SYMONS, DOM THOMAS
  Little Black Boy, The (Blake)
TAYLOR, COLIN
  Downs, The (Galsworthy)
TAYLOR, STANLEY
  Down by the Salley gardens
    (Yeats) ad lib. recorder
    part)
  Sweet was the song (Ballet)
THIMAN, ERIC H.
  I love all graceful things
    (Kathleen Boland)
  Maid of Dunloe, The (Bell)
  Silver birch, The (Nesbit)
  Song-thrush, The (Ann
    Phillips)
  Wee road from Cushendall,
    The
TITHERINGTON, F.
  Sheiling song (Fiona
    McLeod)

TOYE, FRANCIS
  Inn, The (Hilaire Belloc)

WALTON, WILLIAM
  Tritons, The (Drummond)
  Winds, The (Swinburne)

WARLOCK, PETER
  Romance (Stevenson)

WHITTAKER, W. G. (*arr.*)
  Blow the wind southerly

WHYTE, IAN
  I love you, my dear
    (Don Whyte)

WILLIAMS, R. VAUGHAN
  Let us now praise famous
    men
  Songs from *Hugh the Drover*
    (Words by Harold Child):
    Alone and friendless
    Gaily I go to die
    Here on my throne
    Life must be full of care
    Song of the road
    Sweet Little Linnet
    Two Duets (Ah; Love,
      I've Found You;
      Hugh, My Lover)

WRAY, JOHN
  My grief on the sea
    (Douglas Hyde)

ELKIN VOCAL CATALOGUE, 27/28 Soho Square, London W.1.

BAINTON, EDGAR
  The little waves of Breffny

BANTOCK, SIR GRANVILLE
  Adrift
  Babyland
  Boat song of the Isles
  Dream Merchandise

BANTOCK, SIR GRANVILLE
  (*contd.*)
  Emperor, The
  Feast of Lanterns
  From the tomb of an unknown woman
  Garden of Bamboos

BANTOCK, SIR GRANVILLE
(*contd.*)
In the palace
Isles of the seas, The
Land of Promise
Longing
Lullabye
Parting, The
Peach Flower, The
Red Lotus, The
Two roses, The
Waking song
Yung-yang

BENJAMIN, ARTHUR
Man and woman
To Phillis, milking her flock
The Moon
The piper

BRANSON, David
Three Elizabethan Poems:
    The mortal glance
    The wily lover
    Music

BUSH, DR GEOFFREY
Fain would I change that
  note
It was a lover
My true love hath my heart
She hath an eye
Song of praise, A
There is a garden in her face
Three songs of Ben Jonson:
    Echo's lament: The kiss:
    A rebuke
Songs of wonder:
    Here comes a lusty
      wooer
    Polly Pillicote
    Wonder of wonders
    Old Abram Brown
    The little nut-tree

BUSH, DR GEOFFREY (*contd.*)
Four songs from Herrick's
  Hesperides:
    The impatient lover
    Upon the loss of his
      mistress
    To Electra
    Upon Julia's clothes

ELGAR, SIR EDWARD
Two songs:
    Modest and fair: Still to
    be neat
Blue-eyed fairy, The
My old tunes
To the children
When the spring comes
  round

FOGG, ERIC
Devon Maid, The
Empty house, The
Free me from the bonds
Hunting song of the Seeone
  Pack
In the dusky path of a
  dream
It was in May
Lullaby
Ode to a nightingale. *For
baritone string quartet and
harp.*
Peace
Spindrift
Two songs:
    To morning: Laughing
    song
When passion's trance is
  overpast

GIBBS, ARMSTRONG
In youth is pleasure
Love is a sickness
Prayer before sleep

Scott, Cyril (*contd.*)
Have ye seen him pass by?
Huckster, The
Idyll. *For voice and flute.*
Idyllic Fantasy. *For voice, oboe and cello.*
I'll bid my heart be still
Immortality
In a fairy boat
In the valley
Invocation
My captain
My lady sleeps
New Moon, The
Night song
Night wind
Nocturne
Old Loves
Oracle
Osme's Song
Our lady of violets
Pierrot and the Moon maiden
Pilgrim Cranes, The
Prayer, A
Prelude
Rain
Reconciliation
Reflection
Requiem
Rima's call to the Birds. *Scena for soprano and orchestra.*
Roundel of rest, A
Sands of Dee, The
Scotch Lullabye
Sea-fret
Sea-song of Gafran
Serenade
She's but a lassie yet
Song of Arcady, A
Song of Wine, A

Scott, Cyril (*contd.*)
Sorrow
Spring Song
Sundown
Album of Songs for baritone:
A song of London
Arietta
Afterday
A Gift of Silence
Serenade
Villanelle of the Poet's Road
Songs of Old Cathay:
Alone
In absence
A song of wine
Waiting
A picnic

Stanford, Sir Charles
Mopsa

Stewart, D. M.
Four Songs from Last Poems (Housman):
We'll to the woods no more
In the morning
The sigh that heaves the grasses
The first of May

Toye, Francis
Three Songs from Shakespeare:
O mistress mine: Come away Death: Sigh no more
Red-skirted ladies
Sadness
Tell me where is fancy bred

van Someren Godfrey, M.
Ballad of Semmerwater
Birthright
Cradle song

van Someren Godfrey, M.
(*contd.*)
Fear no more the heat of the
    sun
Jean Richepin's Song
Little lady of my heart
Maids who danced their
    shoes into holes

van Someren Godfrey, M.
(*contd.*)
Silent noon
Spring Peace
Why so pale and wan
Warlock, Peter
The passionate shepherd
The sweet o' the year

NOVELLO & CO. LTD, 27/28 Soho Square, London W.1.

Aston, Peter
Five songs of Crazy Jane
    Unacc.

Austin, Frederick
It was a lover and his lass

Bliss, Sir Arthur
Auvergnat
Ballads of the four seasons:
    Spring: Summer: Autumn:
    Winter
A knot of riddles:
    Fish in river
    A bookworm
    Swallows
    A cross of wood
    An oyster
    Sun and Moon
The Enchantress

Bush, Dr Geoffrey
Diaphenia
Lay a garland on my hearse
Now the lusty Spring
When daffodils begin to peer
Weep you no more
What thing is love
Three Elizabethan Songs:
    Fire! Fire!
    Sweet, stay awhile
    Sigh no more ladies

Bruce, M. C.
The shepherdess

Cleghorn Thomson, D.
The Knight of Bethlehem

Dale, Benjamin
Come away, Death
O mistress mine

Du Plessis, Hubert
Five invocations

Dyson, Sir George
Three songs to Julia:
    When I behold
    Sweet be not proud
    Night piece

Elgar, Sir Edward
Angel's Song (Gerontius)
Twilight
Was it some golden star

Farrer, Ernest
Brittany

German, Sir Edward
The Lordling's daughter
It was a lover and his lass
Rolling down to Rio

Hind, John
Mad Maid's song
The Wakening

Joubert, John
Fain would I change that
    note
Love me not for comely grace
My love in her attire
O come soft rest of cares

JOUBERT, JOHN (*contd.*)
  Stay O sweet
  Two invocations:
    To Winter: To Spring

MILFORD, ROBIN
  Laus Deo
  Love on my heart
  So sweet love seemed

MILNER, ANTHONY
  Our Lady's Hours:
    Dawn: Noon: Dusk

MOERAN, E. J.
  Invitation in Autumn
  Four Shakespeare Songs:
    It was a lover
    When daisies pied
    Where the bee sucks
    When icicles hang by the
      wall

MONTGOMERY, BRUCE
  My true love hath my heart
  Four Shakespeare Songs,
    Set 1:
      Full fathom five
      O Mistress mine
      Come away, Death
      Tell me where is fancy
        bred
  Four Shakespeare Songs,
    Set II:
      Take O take
      Who is Sylvia
      When icicles
      Under the greenwood
        tree

PARRY, SIR HUBERT
  And yet I love her
  Ballad of Meshullemuth
    (*Judith*)
  The Child and the twilight
  Crabbed Age and Youth
  Dirge in woods
  Dream Pedlary
  Fairy Town
  God breaketh the battle
    (*Judith*)
  Lady, thou Queen of Israel
    (*Judith*)
  Laird of Cockpen, The
  Lord is long suffering, The
    (*Judith*)
  Love is a bable
  Lover's Garland, A
  Maiden, The
  My true love hath my heart
  My heart is like a singing
    bird
  Sleep
  Stray Nymph of Dian, A
  Three Aspects
  Through the ivory gate
  To Althea, from prison
  When comes my Gwen
  When lovers meet again
  When we two parted
  Whence
  Why so pale and wan
  Witches' wood, The

ROBERTS, MERVYN
  Saint Govan
  The Sentry
  Put a rosebud on her lips

OXFORD UNIVERSITY PRESS, 44 Conduit Street, London W.1.

ALWYN, WILLIAM
  Slum Song (McNiece)

BAIN, MARJORIE
  O gathering Clouds (Bain)

BERKELEY, LENNOX
The Thresher (du Bellay)

BLISS, SIR ARTHUR
Serenade for Baritone and
Overture. *Orch. only.*
Fair is my love (Spenser)
Idyll. *Orch. only.*
In praise of his Daphnis
(Wooton)

BRANSON, DAVID
Look not into my eyes
(Housman)
Phillida (Anon.)

BRITTEN, BENJAMIN
Corpus Christi Carol (Anon.)
The Ship of Rio (de la Mare)

BROWNE, W. DENIS
Diaphenia (Constable)
To Gratiana (Lovelace)

COOKE, ARNOLD
Nocturnes. *Five songs for high
voice, horn and piano.*
The Moon (Shelley)
Returning, we hear the larks
(Rosenberg)
River Roses (Lawrence)
The Owl (Tennyson)
Boat song (Davidson)
Three Songs of Innocence.
For soprano, clarinet and piano.
Piping down the valleys
(Blake)
The Shepherd (Blake)
The Echoing Green (Blake)

DELIUS, FREDERICK
Black roses (Josephson)
Cradle Song (Ibsen)
Homeward way (Vinje)
Indian love song (Shelley)
Let springtime come then
(Jacobsen)

DELIUS, FREDERICK *(contd.)*
Love concealed (Björnson)
Love's philosophy (Shelley)
Nightingale (Henley)
Summer landscape
(Drachmann)
Sweet Venevil (Björnson)
To the Queen of my heart
(Shelley)
Twilight fancies (Björnson)

FISKE, ROGER
Done for (de la Mare)
Miss Cherry (de la Mare)
Old Adam (Beddoes)
Weathers (Hardy)

GIBBS, C. ARMSTRONG
The lamb and the dove
(Rossetti)
A birthday (Rossetti)
Gone were but the winter
(Rossetti)
Philomel (Barnefield)
Lament for Robin Hood
Evening in Summer (Fletcher)
Gipsies (Bashford)

GURNEY, IVOR
Twenty Songs, Vol. 1:
The Singer (Shanks)
The Latmian shepherd
(Shanks)
Black Stitchel (Gibson)
Down by the Salley
Gardens (Yeats)
All night under the moon
(Gibson)
Nine of the clock (Doyle)
You are my sky (Squire)
Ha'nacker Mill (Belloc)
When death to either
shall come (Bridges)
Cathleen ni houliham
(Yeats)

LEY, HENRY G.
    The Lake Isle of Innisfree
        (Yeats)

McCABE, JOHN
    Five Elegies. *For soprano and
        chamber orchestra.*
        Adieu Farewell (Nashe)
        The hour glass (Jonson)
        Eyes that last I saw in
            Tears (Eliot)
        Do not go gentle (Dylan
            Thomas)

MILFORD, ROBIN
    Elegy on that glory of her
        sex (Goldsmith)

MOERAN, E. J.
    Seven poems by James Joyce:
        Strings in the earth
        The merry green wood
        Bright Cap
        The pleasant Valley
        Donny carney
        Rain has fallen
        Now o now in this brown
            land
    In youth is pleasure (Wever)
    Rahoon (Joyce)

MULLINAR, MICHAEL
    I will go with my father
        a-ploughing (Campbell)
    The seas are quiet (Waller)
    An Epitaph (de la Mare)

MURRILL, HERBERT
    To music to becalme his
        fever (Herrick)

ORR, C. W.
    Four songs for high voice.
        Bahnofstrasse (Joyce)
        Requiem (Waddell)
        The time of Roses
            (Hood)

ORR, C. W. (*contd.*)
    Four songs for high voice.
        (*contd.*)
        Since thou O fondest and
            truest (Bridges)
    Five songs from A Shrop-
        shire Lad (Housman):
        With rue my heart is
            laden
        This time of year
        O when I was in love
        Is my team ploughing?
        On your midnight pallet

PETERKIN, NORMAN
    Beatudo solitudo (Dowson)
    The Chaste Wife's reply
        (Giles)
    The Garden of Bamboos
    I heard a piper
    Hours of idleness (Giles)
    I wish and I wish (Campbell)
    A little wind came blowing
        (Peterkin)
    Poems from the Japanese:
        Dew: At the Gate: A
            Farewell: The Guest:
            The forlorn hope
    Sleep white love
        (Maccathnhaoil)
    There is a lady (Ford)
    Under the greenwood tree
        (Shakespeare)

RAWSTHORNE, ALAN
    Carol (Rodgers)
    Two Songs (Fletcher):
        Away delights
        God Lyaeus
    We three merry maidens
        (Anon.)

RAYNOR, JOHN
    Californy Song (Belloc)
    Old Lullaby (Field)

Rowley, Alec
  Pretty Betty (Anon.)
Slater, Gordon
  Green willow (Anon.)
  In time of the breaking of
    Nations (Hardy)

Stevens, Bernard
  Three Songs (Donne):
    Sweetest love I do not
      go
    Go and catch a falling
      star
    The Good-morrow

Tate, Phyllis
  The Quiet Mind (Dyer)
  Nocturne for four voices (Keyes).
    *A chamber cantata for
    soprano, tenor, baritone and
    bass soloists, string quartet,
    double bass, clarinet and
    celesta.*

Thackray, Rupert
  Neglectful Edward (Graves)

Vale, Charles
  Litany to the Holy Spirit
    (Herrick)

Van Dieren, Bernard
  Sonetto VII (Spenser)

Vaughan Williams, Ralph
  Along the Firld. *Eight
    Housman songs for voice and
    violin.*
  Four Last Songs (Ursula
    Vaughan Williams):
    Procis
    Tired
    Hands, eyes and heart
    Menelaus
  In the Spring (Barnes)
  The New Ghost (Shove)

Vaughan Williams, Ralph
  (*contd.*)
  Pilgrim's Progress (Bunyan)
    Watchful's song
    Song of the pilgrims
    The Pilgrim's Psalm
    The song of the leaves of
      life
    The song of Vanity Fair
    Wodcutter's Song
    Bird's Song
  See the chariot at hand
    (Jonson)
  Three Poems of Walt
    Whitman:
    Nocturne
    A clear midnight
    Joy, shipmate, joy
  Ten Blake Songs. *For voice
    and oboe.*
    Infant joy
    A poison tree
    The piper
    London
    The lamb
    The shepherd
    Ah! sunflower
    Cruelty has a human heart
    The divine image
    Eternity
  Three vocalises. *For soprano
    and clarinet.*
    Prelude
    Scherzo
    Quasi Minuetto
  The twilight people
    (O'Sullivan)
  Two Poems by Fredegond
    Shove.
    Motion and stillness
    Four nights
  The Water Mill (Shove)

WALTON, SIR WILLIAM
  Anon. in love (16th and 17th
    Century poems selected by
    Christopher Hassell):
      Fain would I change that
        note
      O stay sweet love
      Lady, when I behold
      My love in her attire
      I gave her cakes and I
        gave her ale
      To couple is a custom
  A Song for the Lord Mayor's
    Show (Devised by Hassell):
      The Lord Mayor's table
        (Jordan)
      Glide gently
        (Wordsworth)
      Wapping old stairs
        (Anon.)
      Holy Thursday (Blake)
      The Contrast (Morris)
      Rhyme (Anon.)
  Three Songs (Edith Sitwell):
    Daphne
    Through gilded trellises
    Old Sir Faulk
  Under the greenwood tree
    (Shakespeare)

WARLOCK, PETER
  A Book of Songs:
    Sleep (Fletcher)
    Pretty ring time
      (Shakespeare)
    Rest sweet nymphs
      (Anon.)
    Sigh no more ladies
      (Shakespeare)
    And wilt thou leave me
      thus (Wyatt)
    Passing by (Anon.)
    Robin Goodfellow
      (Anon.)

WARLOCK, PETER (contd.)
  A Book of songs (contd.)
    Fair and true (Barton)
    The Lover's Maze
      (Campion)
    Cradle Song (Phillip)
    Jillian of Berry (Beaumont
      and Fletcher)
    Twelve Oxen (Anon.)
  After two years (Aldington)
  Autumn twilight (Symons)
  Balulalow (Anon.)
  Consider (Ford)
  The Fox (Blunt)
  The frostbound wood (Blunt)
  Ha'nacker Mill (Belloc)
  I have a garden (Moore)
  Mockery (Shakespeare)
  My lady is a pretty one
    (Anon.). For voice and string
    quartet.
  My Own country (Belloc)
  The night (Belloc)
  Sorrow's lullaby (Beddoes)
  Sweet and twenty (Shakes-
    peare)
  Four English Songs:
    Like to the damask rose
    My thread is spun
    Phillis was a fair maid
    Sigh no more ladies

WISHART, PETER
  Seven Songs:
    Prologue (Shakespeare)
    Complaint (Anon.)
    Dirge (Shakespeare)
    The Mountebank's Song
      (Anon.)
    Serenade (Campion)
    Lullaby of a lover
      (Gascoigne)
    Epilogue (Shakespeare)

STAINER & BELL, 29 Newman Street, London W.1.

BAIRSTOW, EDWARD C.
Orpheus with his lute
(Shakespeare)
Come lovers follow me
(Anon.)
So sweet is she (Jonson)
At Night (Meynell)
To morning (Blake)
The Lonesome Girl (Letts)
The buryin' (Arkell)

BESLY, MAURICE
The mocking Fairy
(de la Mare)

BOUGHTON, RUTLAND
Songs from the *Immortal
Hour:*
Faery Song: The Country
of the Young:
The Song of Creation:
The old Bard's Song:
The Luring song: The
great Lords of Shadow.
Five Celtic Love Songs
'Fiona Macleod':
Green branches: The
daughter of the Sun:
Tragic Lullaby:
Shule agrah: My
Grief

DUNHILL, THOMAS F.
The Wind among the reeds.
*Song cycle for tenor and
orchestra.*
Poems by W. B. Yeats:
To Dectora: The Host
of the Air: The cloths
of Heaven: The
Fiddler of Dooney
Beauty and Beauty (Rupert
Brooke)
The Faun's Song

GIBBS, C. ARMSTRONG
Lullaby (Blake)
Two Songs (de la Mare):
Bluebells
Bunches of Grapes
Five Songs (de la Mare):
The Stranger: The
Linnett: The Moun-
tains: Love in the
Almond Bough: The
Bells

GURNEY, IVOR
Ludlow and Teme. *Song
cycle for tenor and piano
quartet.*
The Western Playland. *Song
cycle for baritone and piano
quartet.*
Captain Stratton's Fancy
(Masefield)
Edward (Percy's Reliques)
Sowing (Edward Thomas)

HOLST, GUSTAV
The Heart Worships
(Buckton)
Weep you no more

HOWELLS, HERBERT
Mally O (Jacobean)
Three Rondeaux:
Roses: A Rondel of
Rest: Her Scuttle Hat
The Restful Branches
(Byrne)

KEEL, FREDERICK
My sweet sweeting (Anon.)
Lullaby (Noyes)
Two songs:
Longing (Arnold): In
prison (Morris)
A poor soul sat a-sighing
(Shakespeare)

Ley, Henry G.
The Rose (Ley)
Far in the Western brook-
land (Housman)
White in the Moon
(Housman)

Rootham, Cyril
A Supplication (Wyatt)
Noel (Gautier)
Three Songs (Thomas Love
Peacock):
Beyond the sea: The
Bramble: The
Greenwood Tree
Two Songs:
I sorrow that the golden
day was dead (Anon.):
The Springtime of
Life (Peacock)
Helen of Kirkconnell
A Boy's Song (Hogg)

Stanford, Sir Charles
Britons, Guard your own
(Tennyson)
Easter snow (Letts)
Irish Skies (Letts)
Heraclitus (Cory)
John Kelly (Letts)
Phoebe (Lodge)
Sea Wrack (O'Neill)
Spring (Tennyson)
The City Child (Tennyson)
The Grand Match (O'Neill)
The King's Highway
(Newbolt)
The Silence (Tennyson)
Song of Asia (Shelley)
The Vision (Tennyson)
Ulster (Wallace)
A Fire of Turf. Song cycle
(Letts):
A fire of Turf: The

F

Stanford, Sir Charles (contd.)
A Fire of Turf. Song cycle
(Letts) (contd.)
chapel on the hill:
Cowslip time: Scared:
Blackberry time: The
fair: The West Wind
A Sheaf of songs from
Leinster. *Poems by W. M.
Letts:*
Grandeur: Thief of the
world: A Soft Day:
Little Peter Morrissey:
The Bold unbiddable
child: Irish Skies
Cushendall Song cycle
(Stevenson):
Ireland: Did you ever?:
Cushendall: The
Crow: Daddy long
legs: How does the
wind blow: Night
Songs from The Elfin Pedlar
(Helen Douglas Adam):
Book 1:
Two Little Stars
The Pedlar
Little Snowdrops
The piper of Spring
Speedwell
The dream Ship
Book 2:
Summer
What do you see?
The piper
The Secret Place
Night
The Dustman
The Songs of the Fleet. *For
baritone solo and chorus.*
(Newbolt):
Sailing at Dawn: The

STANFORD, SIR CHARLES (*contd.*)
 The songs of the Fleet
 (*contd.*)
  Middle Watch: The
  song of the Sou'-
  wester: The little
  Admiral: Farewell
 Bible Songs. *For voice and
 organ:*
  A song of Freedom: A
  Song of Trust: A Song
  of Hope: A song of
  Peace: A Song of
  Battle: A Song of
  Wisdom

VAUGHAN WILLIAMS, RALPH
 Five Mystical Songs (Herbert)
  Easter: I Got me
  flowers: Love bade
  me welcome: The
  Call: Antiphon

WALTHEW, RICHARD
 Diaphenia (Constable)
 England (Johnson)
 Three of us (Anon.)

WALTHEW, RICHARD (*contd.*)
 Our Lady's children
  (Donaldson)
 Five Songs from Thackeray:
  The garret: The age of
  Wisdom: The king on
  the tower: Sorrows of
  Werther: The
  mahogany tree

WOOD, CHARLES
 Fineen the Rover (Joyce)
 Kate of Garnavilla (Lysaght)
 My Wicklow mountains
  (Graves)
 Pastheen Fionn (Ferguson)
 The enchanted valley
  (Graves)
 The forester's complaint
  (Ferguson)
 The High Caul cap (McCall)
 The sea singer (Graves)
 The winding banks of Erne
  (Allingham)
 Tim an Irish Terrier (Letts)
 Irish Countryside Songs in
  three volumes

List of Handel's Operatic Arias

Rinaldo
Lascia ch'io Pianga
Il vostro maggio

Teseo
Ricordati, o bella
Vieni torna
Le luci del mio bene

Flavio
Benche povera donzella

Siroe
O placido il mare

Partenope
Voglio dire al mio lesoro
Si, scherza sempre Amor

Guilio Cesare
Piangero la sorte mia
Empio, diro tu sei

Rodelinda
Conrauco mormorio
Confusa si mira
Ritorna, o Caro

Scipione
Pensa, o bella

Alessandro
Lusinghe piu care

Admeto
Ah, si moro

Riccardo Primo
Caro, vieni a me

Tolomeo
Voi dolce aurette al cor
Stille amare

Radamisto
Ombra cara

Ottone
La profonde vie dell' onde
Ritorna o dolce amore
Affanni del pensier
Del minacciar del vento

Sosarme
Rendi 'l sereno al ciglio

Lothario
Per salvarti, idolo mio

Orlando
Sorge, infausta
Verdi allori

Alcina
Verdi prati
Pensa a che geme d'amor

Arminio
Vado a morir

Faramondo
Sento che un giusto sdegno

Poro
Dov' e?
Son confusa pastorella

Ariodante
Volate amori

Atalanta
Come alla totorella

Berenice
Si tra i ceppi

Serse
Ombra mai fui
Caro voi siete

Index